WHY
WORSHIP?

WHY WORSHIP?

(FIVE BIBLICAL RESPONSES)

WAYNE BERRY

WordCrafts Press

Why Worship?
Copyright © 2025
Wayne Berry

Hardback ISBN: 978-1-967649-14-3
Paperback ISBN: 978-1-967649-15-0

Cover concept and design by Jonathan Grisham for Grisham Designs.

Published by WordCrafts Press
Cody, Wyoming 82414
www.wordcrafts.net

Contents

Part One

The First Commandment..1
The Precept, Process, and Practice of Consecration.............3
Idolatrous Behavior vs. Sacrificial/Holy Service.....................11
The Cycle of Hope 13
The Channel of Grace..14
Destiny and Legacy 19

Part Two

Are Y'all Breathin'? 21
Worship on the Wind (A Personal Revelation).......................29
Reconsidering Worship 34
Distinct, Not Separate...35
The Principle of First Mention 41
In the Beginning 43
The Breath of Life 44

Part Three

A Congregational Response 49
Why Do We Sing in Church? 50
The Importance of Continuous Massive Praise 54
Praise Is Where God Lives 55
Enthroning God..59

Part Four

Worshippers Will Worship 71
The Real Deal 72
Spirit and Truth 74
Who's Seeking Who?..76
Kingdom Coordinates (Proximity and Intimacy) 82
Disclaimer(S) 84
Embodiment In Action...92

Part Five

Our Reasonable Acts Of Service..95
Serving, Singing, and Sojourning...99
Doing What's Expected (Response-ability) 109
To the Least of These 115
No Servant Is Above Their Master 120

Addendum

Sojourner's Song Source...124
Concerning Franchised Worship..135
Treasures Old and New..136
Hanging Up Our Harps 138
Looking at Lament..139
Silent Worship..144
The Pursuit of Presence 146

DEDICATIONS

To Father God, the Creator of life (Gen. 1:26), Jesus Christ, my Lord, Savior, and life sustained (Acts 17:28; Rom. 8:34), the Holy Ghost, guide, comforter, sanctifier, and the force behind the source (Acts 1:8); my family; Kingdom confidants; friends; associates; cohorts; co-defendants and…

…to paraphrase Bob Dylan as he so eloquently opined in his song "Chimes of Freedon," this is for everyone in the whole wide world who is hung-up, strung-out, misused, muddled, ill-used, harrassed, and worse.

"Now may the Lord of peace himself give you peace at all times in every way. The Lord be with you all,"
                                                            ~2 Thess. 3:16

There is only one verse in Scripture where Jesus states what is to be Priority #1 for all those who purpose to follow Him:

> *"Seek first the kingdom of God and His righteousness, and all these things will be added to you,"*
> ~*Mt. 6:33*

The first phrase in that verse is what pointed me toward the pathway this book follows. Along the way, there were four aspects I saw as foundational to my postulations:

1. Seeking the kingdom of God and His righteousness are not two separate things. They are distinct pursuits toward the same goal.
2. What does *seek* mean?
3. What does *kingdom* mean?
4. What does *righteousness* mean?

"We are to discipline ourselves to '*seek first the Kingdom of God and His righteousness.*' This focus must take precedence over absolutely everything. We must never allow anything, whether deed or desire, to have that place of central importance,"
~Richard Foster, *Freedom of Simplicity*
Harper & Row, 1981

To live in obedience to the charge of that text requires consideration for each of those points. I see no way of placing Jesus' directive at the top of my "to do" list without some extensive pondering.

I began my Kingdom quest (in earnest) some forty-five years ago. Strong's Bible Concordance provides some basic trail markers I came across in my sojourn:

1. **Seek:** To worship; to desire, endeavor, enquire (for or about).
2. **Kingdom:** A realm of royalty. From a word meaning a foundation of power; a sovereign king or kingship.
3. **Righteousness:** Equity (of character or act); holy, just. From a word meaning right or just (in principle, decision or its execution).

The initial question, *Why Worship?* is rooted in my personal quest to establish Matthew 6:33 as first and foremost in my life. I'm still following that trail.

> My first step as a disciple is to constantly be learning from Jesus how to live in the Kingdom of God now—my real life, the one I am living. Not just in church or on "religious" occasions. That is what he meant by saying, "Seek above all the Kingdom of God and his kind of righteousness." (They, of course, are inseparable.)
>
> ~Dallas Willard, *The Great Omission*
> Harper One, 2006

Here's the essence of that quest, in seed form:

The fruits of anything living come directly from its roots. Before it can manifest, it must first have a motivational dynamic that activates (births) it. The conception (the *why*) must exist prior to the reality being formed, expressed, and experienced.

Without addressing the *whys*, all the other aspects (manifestations) of worship are theologically random. That doesn't mean that they aren't important—they certainly are—but only in a subordinate sense. The context of a subject provides a container for the content, from which all other inner-related topics can be considered, articulated, and implemented. In that sense, this book is the context-container for the *why* content.

Thus, my primary purpose is to focus on five specific *whys* of worship intentionally and purposefully, with the following verse in mind:

> *"There is a river whose *streams make glad the city of God, the holy habitation of the Most High,"*
>
> ~*Ps. 46:4*

*One river with multiple streams.

Where the Water Is
~Ps. 65:9

If the well where you drink runs dry
And you don't know how or why
Come to where the water is
If you're lost in a barren land
And all you can see is sand
Come to where the water is

And God will bless you beyond measure
He's concerned about your welfare
Out of your innermost being
Living what will flow like a fountain
If you'll just come, come to where the water is

If the well where you drink runs dry
And all you can do is cry
Come to where the water is
If you're trapped in the wilderness
You're still a child of His
(Come on) Come to where the water is
The stream of the Lord is full (Repeat)

~W. Berry, See & Say Songs, BMI

DISCLAIMER

As you read through this sacrificial offering (Rom. 12:1 and Col. 3:17), you'll likely notice several verses and passages from Scripture are repeated. That's not an oversight that took place during the editing process. It's been done on purpose. I used a sort of *intentional redundancy* as I was developing the overall work. Over the years of my sojourn up to Zion (see Ps. 84:5–7), I've noticed that many so-called followers of Christ have disregarded several principles, precepts, and practices presented in the Word. These aspects no longer seem of fundamental worth, having been relegated to the wayside as mere footnotes in a faith-walk. A lack of ethical kingdom consecration and disciplined obedience has made fulfilling the *Ministry of Reconciliation as Ambassadors for Christ* seem unnecessary, virtually impossible, or both (see 2 Cor. 5:18–21). I've tried to line up my life as a witness for Jesus, with my declaration(s) of what I understand and believe Biblical spirituality to be. This project is intended as a testimonial in the process of being conformed into the image of Christ (Rom. 8:29), my Lord and Savior—to the glory of the Father, through the Presence, power, and purpose of the Holy Ghost. (See Acts 1:8.)

> *Let the words of my mouth and the meditation of my heart be acceptable in your sight, O Lord, my rock and my redeemer.*
>
> *~Psalm 19:14*

Pre-Introduction

And he said to them, "Therefore every scribe who has been
trained for the kingdom of heaven is like a master of a house,
who brings out of his treasure what is new and what is old."
                                        ~Mt.13:52 ESV

This book contains treasures, both old and new. It's an assortment
of Scriptural renderings, insightful (and impactful) quotes, instruc-
tive directives, and prophetic insights—past, present, and future.
Think of the pages as shelves in a general store. Perhaps you'll find
things herewith that you've been seeking, or that you didn't even
know you were looking for.

He said, "Then you see how every student well-trained
in God's kingdom is like the owner of a general store who
can put his hands on anything you need, old or new, exactly
when you need it."
                                        ~Mt.13:52 The Message Bible

INTRODUCTION

This work is rooted in a blog post that I drafted in April of 2010. It was inspired by a song I'd heard almost twenty years prior. The lyrics reminded me of a 1952 book by J.B. Phillips, which in chain rection form, led to my blog post. I've since been traveling along a pathway that began some seventy-three years ago (see Ps. 84:5–7).

Here's the original blog entry:

> Thursday, April 1, 2010
>
> Some 15+ years ago, I came across a wonderful song by Lynn DeShazo entitled "Be Magnified." The opening line drove me to my knees.
>
> "I have made You too small in my eyes. Oh Lord, forgive me."
>
> That phrase lined up in my memory with a book I'd read several years prior to hearing Lynn's song. It was titled *Your God Is Too Small*, written by J.B. Phillips. Such a concept is humbling to consider.
>
> The idea of viewing God from a narrowed, and shallow perspective can create a seemingly insurmountable problem for saints both individually as well as corporately. Such a limited vista of God and His kingdom has stifled believers and derailed numbers of fellowships over the years.
>
> There are several things that can cause one's perspective to turn inwardly myopic. Addressing them would take far more time and consideration than is appropriate in a format such as this one. So, for now, I'll only comment on one in particular which tends to try and squeeze God into our little boxes of belief. In specific, I'm speaking of our worship theology or lack thereof—the study of why we believe as we do about matters related

to the Father, Son, and Holy Ghost. The stuff of God's kingdom.

"Without a solid foundational theology, worship becomes an exercise in self-expression."

~Timothy Pierce, *Enthroned on Our Praise*
B&H Academic, 2008

Here's what I see taking place within our churches in the U. S. and throughout the nations-at-large. In the process of going contemporary we've learned the how and what of worship well, but we've discarded much of the why. In other words, we've figured out how worship should manifest in our congregations, and we know what to do to (seemingly) make that happen—but we no longer give much thought to why we worship.

In essence we've allowed our "too small" view of God to restrict our ability to reach out beyond ourselves and our limited and temporal understanding of Him. In doing so, we are (in a sense) restraining the Lord's ability to increase within and among us. The end result of such a process is that much of the mystery of the kingdom and the world of wonder(s) that life in the Spirit affords has been diminished.

We need a bigger God than the one we currently worship. So, for the sake of enlargement consider the following passage from Scripture:

He spreads the skies over unformed space, hangs the earth out in empty space. He pours water into cumulus cloud-bags and the bags don't burst. He makes the moon wax and wane, putting it through its phases. He draws the horizon out over the ocean, sets a boundary between light and darkness. The thunder crashes and rumbles in the skies.

*Listen! It's God raising his voice! By his power he stills sea storms, by his wisdom he tames sea monsters. With one breath he clears the sky, with one finger he crushes the sea serpent. **And this is only the beginning, a mere whisper of his rule.***

~Job 26:5–14 MSG, emphasis added

The process of pursuing (seeking after) God's kingdom and His righteousness is varied and wide-ranging. In my own journey, I came across a particular verse that sheds light on one way of seeking that's well worth pondering. Hebrews 11:6 says, *"But without faith it is impossible to please him: for he that cometh to God must believe that he is, and that he is a rewarder of them that diligently seek him," (KJV).*

In looking at Strong's Bible Concordance, the word *seek* in this verse isn't the same as in Matthew 6:33. In Hebrews 11:6, it means to search out, investigate, crave, demand, worship, and to do so diligently. This definition is more nuanced than the text in Matthew, where *seek* means to worship, plot, desire, endeavor, and enquire (for or about). These two definitions are compatible, but they are not the same. I consider them to be distinct in their meanings and applications.

The Hebrews 11:6 application carries a little more weight and provides a little more insight into the process of seeking. But there's another aspect to this verse that's unique in and of itself. The word *diligently* is the exact same word as *seek*, with the exact same definition. Therefore, the verse could read, a rewarder of those that seek (and keep seeking) or, a rewarder of those who are doubly diligent in their seeking.

When I combined the directive of Jesus to *seek* in Matthew 6:33, with the Hebrews 11:6 text, it appeared that the faith component it mentions—combined with the application of being doubly diligent—offers an extra incentive as a reward of some sort. What that reward is, or how (or when) it is received, I do not know.

However, that's how those two narratives seem to be linked together.

Everything I've stated thus far provides the context for the content of what's to follow. Whatever the reward is, I'm committed toward securing it. However, I'm not after that as a sort of prize for my efforts. Rather, my pursuits are based on following the Hebrew 11:6 directive.

> *"And whatever you do, in word or deed, do everything in the name of the Lord Jesus, giving thanks to God the Father through him,"*
>
> ~Col. 3:17

I've spent the last forty-five years pondering, processing and practicing what Jesus said/says is to be the #1 Priority for *all* those who consider themselves to be his followers.

> *"Seek first the kingdom of God and His righteousness…"*
>
> ~Mt. 6:33

In the last five years or so, I've noticed something regarding the subject of worship. Much of our theology, rhetoric, preaching, teaching, commentary, printed material, and podcasts address the *who, what, how, where,* and *when* of it, but far less attention is given to the *whys.* That observation is what birthed this book. In what follows, I'm not considering worship from a wide-ranging broad-based religious perspective. My target is much narrower. What I'm aiming at is two-fold:

1. Why did God create the concept of worship in the first place?
2. Why do Christians worship?

Biblically speaking, there is a plethora of reasons that could be used to answer these two questions. I've chosen to offer only five in specific. Why so? Because that's what the Holy Ghost directed me to do.

"But without faith it is impossible to please Him, for he who comes to God must believe that He is, and that He is a rewarder of those who diligently seek Him,"

~Heb.11:6

This is part of my due diligence...

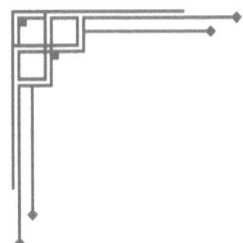

Part One

THE FIRST COMMANDMENT

Thou shalt have no other gods *before me.
                                    ~Deuteronomy 5:7

*The marginal notes in the NASB use the word *besides* instead of *before.*

This verse provides *the* foundational context regarding why we worship—what our purpose is or should be. It is, after all, the first Commandment presented in Scripture, and given to humankind. The essence of God-worship is clearly stated in that narrative. Jehovah was/is being intentional about placing worship as Priority #1 in the Old Testament. In turn, we should be equally intentional as to *why* we are to worship.

No Other God

~Deut. 5:7

No other god can claim the place You hold in my heart
No other god can speak the words of life to my soul

CHORUS:
All the praise I have, I offer up to Thee
In worship of the Most High God
In worship of the Most High God
In worship of the Most High God

No other god can break the bond You hold to my heart
No other god can sweep away the night's dark glow

BRIDGE:
You are holy, and worthy of all praise
You are righteous, and just in all Your ways
You are faithful, compassionate and true
God Almighty, I give myself to You
                    ~W. Berry, See & Say Songs, BMI

Right here at the top, I'll address what I believe is the fundamental *why* related to the topic of worship.

The bedrock rooting of Deuteronomy 5:7 is worship. It has to do with not only obeying the command from the Creator of life itself, but also the *why*—because He said so. In addition, a basic understanding of how such worship is to be done is necessary, to be able to follow through with yielding to the charge expressed in the text. I believe that the *how* is directly linked to the principle, process, and practice of consecration. What follows is my exposition on that topic.

The Precept, Process, and Practice of Consecration

Some twenty-plus years ago, I had the honor of studying under the direction of Professor Robert Weber through the Institute for Worship Studies (IWS). As a student I picked up a teaching tool from him that has served me well over the years. Often in his classes, he used what he called a "working definition" when he wanted his students to focus in on a certain word or topic. Here's how it worked:

He would explain to the class that he wanted everyone to consider his "working definition" as a point of agreement in terms of understanding or belief. He didn't care if the students had a different idea of their own (in terms of meaning), nor did he necessarily intend for them to believe as he did.

However, for the sake of a unified understanding, he expected the students to accept his "working definition" to move everyone along together as he taught. Following that precedent, here's my "working definition" for *consecration:*

> *Consecration is the setting apart of any person, place, or thing for acts of holy service.*

The ponderings to follow will all be unpacked out of that definition.

The first thing I have to say about how the process of consecration works is that we must begin by determining what acts of holy service are. Why? Because you cannot consecrate acts of unholy service. Doing so would be a contradiction in terms. I suppose you could approach this by saying that you'd first have to determine what unholy acts are, and then not do them. Otherwise, the very act of consecration would be compromised.

Are you tracking what I'm saying here?

If not, perhaps you should allow yourself a little pondering space while you re-read what I've just said. Having a grasp on this first point will have a direct bearing on what follows in this chapter.

The best example of consecration from a personal point of view would be what takes place when someone surrenders their life to Christ by accepting Him as Savior. When that happens, almost everyone who comes to salvation prays a prayer which basically says something like, "I give my life to you, Lord." They then receive reconciliation through their act of consecration (2 Cor. 5:17–21). Even if they're never heard the word or understood the concept, what they have done is to set themself apart for holy service to God, through Christ's Spirit, which is exactly what it means to be consecrated. (Also see Rom. 12:1 in The Message Bible, and Col. 3:17.)

However, that formative first step of consecration isn't all there is to living a consecrated life (or lifestyle). Step one leads you through the doorway into God's kingdom, but it doesn't grow you up into it. There are many more steps ahead we are called to take regarding consecration before we reach a level of spiritual maturity in matters of service unto our Lord.

I'm going to continue unpacking an understanding about this process. But, for the sake of clarity, I need to consider an aspect of how Biblical language can sometimes be confusing.

In the King James Version (and a few other translations) the words *sanctification* and *consecration* are sometimes interchangeable. On occasion one-word can be used instead of the other, and vice

4

versa. That can be confusing if you haven't worked with both topics as distinct from one another.

Having handled both topics for several years of study, and practical application, I have no problem or issue with how the words are interchanged—because I see a difference, and I understand how that difference can (or should) be considered. Let me explain by using a scriptural example:

In Joshua 3:5 we read that Joshua is giving the wilderness children a directive to follow. He says to the people, *"consecrate yourselves, for tomorrow the Lord will do wonders among you."* Clearly that verse is placing the responsibility upon the people to set themselves apart. To do so requires something of them on an individual and personal level. The holy service that Joshua is calling the people to offer is meant to prompt them to make themselves available to God.

Therefore, you could say that consecration was their work in the context of that verse. Thereafter (by extension), it becomes our work too, *if* we are purposed and intentional about offering ourselves to God through our own act(s) of consecration.

On the other hand, we find that the principle or practice of sanctification in the New Testament is the work of the Holy Spirit (2 Thess. 2:13, 1 Pet. 1:2). Such a process—empowerment by and implemented through the Holy Spirit—is the very process by which He conforms us into the character, nature, and personality of our Lord, Christ Jesus.

The Spirit does the work we cannot do ourselves. We cannot convert or conform our own lives into the likeness of our Savior, for that is one of the major roles the Spirit was sent here to accomplish. Let me say it this way:

The Holy Spirit sanctifies what we offer Him to sanctify through our personal and individual act(s) of consecration. The two steps work in conjunction with each other. They are (in a Biblical sense) necessary for the process to work properly. We do our work, and the Spirit does His. Consider all that from this perspective: *"Therefore humble yourselves under the mighty hand of God, that He may exalt you at the proper time…"* (1 Pet. 5:6a, NASB 1995). It is our job to humble ourselves through the process and practice of consecration. It is God's job (through the Spirit, and on His terms) to exalt us. If we insist on doing God's job, then He has no choice but to do ours.

Selah (Pause & ponder.)

To further clarify what I'm saying, consider this:

In the King James Version, Joshua 3:5 uses the word *sanctify* instead of *consecration.* That's where the language can get confusing. If consecration is our job (as Joshua clearly states that it is), then how are we to sanctify ourselves since the New Testament clearly states that to be the work of the Holy Spirit?

You may not agree with my theological approach in this matter. But, to proceed from here, I encourage you to withhold any judgment until I develop my pondering further.

Let's look at Joshua 3:5 with a little more attention to the details it provides us:

Joshua tells the people to consecrate themselves in preparation for the wonders God is going to do the following day—tomorrow (KJV). So, when are the people to perform their act(s) of consecration? The answer to that is found in a word that isn't in the text but is nonetheless implied in it. The verse could/should read, *"Consecrate yourselves (today), for tomorrow God will do wonders among you."*

The actions required for consecration to be in place are to take place *prior* to the need for it to be established. Joshua is saying that God's movement among the people (His awesome deeds) will take place tomorrow—after the people have consecrated themselves. I take that to mean that not being spiritually prepared for God to move prior to Him doing so has a direct bearing on being in on the action when He starts to move. In other words, we can miss out on at least some portion of God's will as He moves (in Presence, power, and purpose), if we are not first prepared spiritually for such movement. I would call that a lack of consecration, wouldn't you?

There are theological exceptions to the practice of consecration being solely our responsibility. However, the exception doesn't cancel out someone's individual or personal obligation of preparing for the process. No. Rather, it merely modifies it. I'll show you what I mean by looking at Jeremiah 1:5 which says, *"Before I formed you in the womb I knew you, and before you were born, I consecrated you…"*

In this verse, we see that Jehovah is in fact the one doing the consecrating. You could say that He is the Consecrator. So, that does offer us a view for a modified manner of consecration taking place; the modification being that someone other than us can set us apart for acts of holy service. However, the fulfillment of such an action (by someone other than us) does not complete the process. If we are not willing to walk in and serve out of an act of consecration spoken over us, or to us, then the process is short circuited altogether.

We are never exempt from following through with the responsibility placed upon us in matters related to yielded and obedient service. The entire process places two specific questions before us which we alone must answer:

1. Are we willing and available to present ourselves through acts of consecration, which we do of our own free will?
2. Are we willing and available to carry out our own acts of consecration when someone in authority places a charge (calling) on, or over, us?

Answering both questions in the affirmative enables us to be available to serve God's kingdom in whatever ways He may call us to. Answering either one of them with a *no* can/will block our availability to willingly cooperate with what God is doing, and when He's doing it. I personally view the entire subject of consecration as being one of the most basic, yet overlooked, misunderstood, and rarely taught or preached about subjects within the church today.

Now, let's look at another example from Scripture that

provides us with an even clearer example of how this process of consecration is meant to work:

Turn to 2 Chronicles 29 and read the entire chapter, then we'll examine it together...

I'll make two observations before our examination begins: Firstly, I consider this chapter to be the best Biblically-based model for how the process of consecration should work. Secondly, learning how to apply what it teaches regarding obedience and servanthood can be life changing in terms of our relationship to the Father, Son, and Holy Ghost.

In verse three, we are given the context for what's about to take place. Hezekiah passes down a directive to begin refurbishing the *"house of the Lord."* If you'll recall the "working definition" I mentioned earlier, it contained three areas of consideration for consecration: Person, Place, and/or Thing. Clearly the *"house of the Lord"* is a place. So, what's being addressed is how to take the necessary steps for consecration (by setting it apart for holy service).

In verse four, Hezekiah assigns two groups of people to carry out his wishes—Priests and Levites. These two groups are chosen because they are (or should be) properly trained and equipped to serve, based on their consecration. They not only have a historical foundation for doing so, but they also understand the principles and the practices of living a consecrated life in service to, and before, the Lord. Their spiritual heritage and their way of living have positioned them to conduct the works of service they are now charged with.

From verses five through nineteen we see the specific details of what needs to be done to restore the Temple to a place made holy and pure for the ministry. In verses twenty through thirty-six, an application of consecration is presented in detail:

Having assigned the workers and the work to be carried out (vs.3–19), the next stage of restoration begins with Hezekiah entering the house of the Lord, accompanied by the city leaders —the princes. Together they start implementing the historically established protocol necessary to reactivate temple worship (vs. 21–24). From there, things begin to get very interesting as the story continues to unfold.

DISCLAIMER: I'm going to render the remainder of this chapter using a more contemporary language, to provide a perspective that might help relate to how acts of consecration can be understood in today's world. To do so, keep in mind how I unpacked Joshua 3:5 a few pages back:

Consecration is (or can be) required before the need for it arises. The reason for that—the rationale—is to enable those who are consecrated to be readily available and potentially active in any movement(s) that are being initiated by God, or by those who are serving in obedient leadership on His behalf.

The narrative continues in verse twenty-three: Hezekiah stations the Levites who are trained to serve as the worship team band, in accordance with their giftings and their anointings. (They are not the priests. The priests have an entirely different role to play in this scenario.) The Levites described here are the in-house musicians and singers. Such positioning is based on directives established under the guidance of David. (For background, read 1 Chronicles 15. There you'll find the prototypical foundation that still applies in the so-called worship departments of many contemporary church services of today.)

In verses twenty-six through twenty-eight, church liturgy (i.e. service flow) begins, based on the *how, when,* and *where* of historical enactment. The *why* of all that's taking place is based on the ongoing directive (fulfillment) of Deuteronomy 5:7. (At least that's a linkage that I can easily make.) However, beginning in verse thirty-one, a major shift in protocol starts to unfold.

To set up what follows, re-read 2 Chronicles 29:5–11. Those verses clearly establish the context for everything that's about to happen. Pay close attention to verse eleven, which says, *"My sons, do not be negligent now, for the Lord has chosen you to stand before Him, to minister to Him, and to be His ministers and burn incense,"* (NIV).

In verse thirty-one, Hezekiah speaks directly to those who have gathered—the assembled congregation of worshippers. Thirty-two and thirty-three provide specifications regarding the sacrifices being offered. What happens next presents the Biblical reason for the foundational underpinning of consecration...

> *But the priests were too few and could not flay all the burnt offerings, so until other priests had consecrated themselves, their brothers the Levites helped them, until the work was finished—for the Levites were more upright in heart than the priests in consecrating themselves. Besides the great number of burnt offerings, there was the fat of the peace offerings, and there were the drink offerings for the burnt offerings. Thus, the service of the house of the Lord was restored. And Hezekiah and all the people rejoiced because God had provided for the people, for the thing came about suddenly.*
>
> ~2 Chronicles 29:34–36

Here's my modern-day rendering of verses thirty through thirty-six:

The musicians and the singers all showed up ready to lead the congregation in corporate worship. They had their instruments, amps, effects pedals, keyboards, drum-booth-containment-system, and multiple vocal mics. They knew their jobs, and they had taken appropriate steps to consecrate themselves for the events that were unfolding. But then, suddenly, Hezekiah (and most everyone else) realized a major problem was beginning to take place. Due to an extended time of inactivity, the priests had become lax in their preparation for service. It hadn't occurred to them that so many people were going to enter the sanctuary with the intention of bringing their offerings. To do so, the role of overseeing that process was the responsibility of the consecrated priests.

To facilitate what was required, Hezekiah decided to break

protocol by drafting the musician and singers into a service that wasn't theirs to perform. Although they were prepared to carry out the duties that they were gifted and anointed for, they were now being called on to function in the service of priestly work.

What qualified them wasn't their natural abilities; rather, their acts of consecration positioned them in roles that they had never even considered taking part in. As a result, the *place* was set apart, as was their equipment (things), and themselves (their personages).

Consecration made a way for them to be directly involved in what God was doing at that moment in real-time. It is a perfect example of what was addressed in Joshua 3:5. This Biblically-based historical story provides a practical model for how the process of consecration is designed and intended to operate in matters of worship—personally as well as corporately. And that's one of the *whys* of worship, linked to consecration and rooted in the commandment of Deuteronomy 5:7, which began this chapter.

Idolatrous Behavior vs. Sacrificial/Holy Service

Deuteronomy 5:7 commands the redeemed of the Lord not to have other gods. Such idols are identified at the beginning with a small *g* (meaning lesser), and an *s* at the end (meaning plural or multiple). The text is stating that other gods [in fact] do exist, but they should not be gods we worship, yield to, or serve.

Psalm 135 describes what lesser gods are like, and what effect they have on those who follow them:

> *The idols of the nations are silver and gold, the work of human hands. They have mouths, but do not speak; they have eyes, but do not see; they have ears, but do not hear, nor is there any breath in their mouths. Those who make them become like them, so do all who trust in them.*
> ~Psalm 135:15–18 KJV

The New Testament counterbalance is stated in Romans, showing the effect of obeying (yielding to) lesser gods:

> *Do you not know that if you present yourselves to anyone as obedient slaves, you are slaves of the one whom you obey, either of sin, which leads to death, or of obedience, which leads to righteousness?*
>
> ~Romans 6:16

Colossians 3:17 charges followers of Christ with offering all they say and do to God. This New Testament directive links back to the Old Testament command given in Deuteronomy 5:7.

Worship and Praise are external expressions of internal reality. They are not separate things. Rather, they are distinct in form, substance, and manifestation. Think of them as two sides to the same coin. In their distinctness, they share two key aspects:

1. Internal residence
2. External expression

The internal residence of the Spirit is necessary for external expression(s) to take place (see Psalm 139:5–7 and 1 Corinthians 3:17). You really can't have one without the other. If outward signs of worship and/or praise take place without first being authentically alive and active in the heart, such expressions will be shallow at best, or false (disingenuous) displays.

I am not prepared (or qualified) to wade out into the deep waters of theological study regarding God's Providence. Such hermeneutical exegesis is way above my pay grade. Suffice it to say that in matters of Praise and Worship, outer expression really must begin with inner reality, guided by the Lord Himself.

> *Israel, you have no right to argue with your Creator. You are merely a clay pot shaped by a potter. The clay doesn't ask, "Why did you make me this way? Where are the handles?" Children don't have the right to demand of*

their parents, "What have you done to make us what we are?" I am the Lord, the Creator, the holy God of Israel. Do you dare question me about my own nation or about what I have done?
~Isaiah 45:9–11 CEV

Simply stated, as an act of worship (Col. 3:17), I trust Him. Here's what I mean by that:

Trust becomes activated as an expression of belief, based on faith. Faith manifests out of hope, and hope flows directly from grace, requested and appropriated from the throne of grace. Here's how I unpack this process.

The Cycle of Hope

Grace is appropriated directly from the throne of grace. (Heb. 4:16)

Hope flows out of grace. (2 Thess. 2:16)

Faith manifests directly from hope. (Heb. 11:1)

Trust is the active result of faith. (1 Tim. 4:10)

"Grace is the divine favor of God's empowering Presence, enabling me to be who He created me to be, so I can do what He calls me to do."
~James Ryle

Using Ryle's definition of grace as the "working definition," notice the phrase "what He calls me to do." There are several things that followers of Christ are called to do. However, there are two in specific that seem to be essential:

1. We are given the ministry of reconciliation (our job description). (2 Cor. 5:18)
2. We are to serve as ambassadors for Christ (our job title). (2 Cor. 5:20)

13

Grace is the component that empowers and enables both aspects to function properly. The solicitation and appropriation of grace makes that possible (see Heb. 4:16).

The book of Hebrews is written to a collective group of believers (a congregation of sorts). The directive is meant to be applied to all among that grouping. However, each person can apply it directly to their own lives as well. There is nothing in the text that prohibits individuals from appropriating grace for others to help in their time of need. So, the text works in two ways:

1. Acquisition of grace individually
2. Distribution of grace collectivity (by extension)

The Channel of Grace

Once again, I'll begin with my working definition of grace:

"Grace is the divine favor of God's empowering Presence, enabling me to be who He created me to be, so I can do what He calls me to do."

~James Ryle

I see three basic ways of receiving grace:

1. As a gift, salvific grace. (Heb. 11:1)
2. By solicitation (requested), appropriation (for us), and by extension on behalf of others (Heb. 4:16). When we appropriate grace for ourselves through solicitation, we can thereafter request it on behalf of others with the intention of distributing it as the need(s) arise. By doing so, we become grace agents—or perhaps graced agents.
3. Any and every way that God chooses to impart it, whenever, wherever, and to whomever He chooses. Some theologians call that "common grace." I think that phrase works well.

If you'll consider grace as flowing like a river, there are three

14

conduits it passes through, from the throne of grace to humanity. After it's released from the throne of *grace* (Heb. 4:16), it passes through Conduit #1 which is *hope* (2 Thess. 2:16). From there it flows out into Conduit #2 which is *faith* (Heb. 11:1). Passing through there, it arrives via Conduit #3 which is *trust* (1 Tim. 4:10).

Following that line of reasoning, I suggest that you undertake an earnest examination of hope. If you do, ask the Holy Ghost to impart insight and understanding to you through the process.

A supporting passage for *The Cycle of Hope* dynamic is found in 2 Corinthians 1:3–5:

> *Blessed be the God and Father of our Lord Jesus Christ, the Father of mercies and God of all comfort, who comforts us in all our *affliction, so that we may be able to comfort those who are in any affliction, with the comfort with which we ourselves are comforted by God. For as we share abundantly in Christ's sufferings, so through Christ we share abundantly in comfort too.*

*Affliction is translated *tribulation* in the King James Version, meaning anguish, burdened, persecution, trouble.

The text says that we are to comfort those who are in affliction (tribulation) with the same comfort that God comforts us. This directive is outworked in Hebrews 4:16, which is where the *Cycle of Hope* begins. From there the cycle continues, as discussed earlier: grace flows out as hope; hope manifests as faith; and faith is implemented as trust.

If followers of Christ were to put this "Cycle" into practice (daily) for themselves—and for others—humanity would be drastically altered (altared).

Such an implementation by those who are *"hidden with Christ in God"* (Col. 3:3) would be functioning in their roles as *"ministers of reconciliation* and *ambassadors for Christ"* in the manner to which they are called. Such a calling would help to reach the goal stated in Hebrews 2:10 which says, *"For it was fitting that he, for whom and by whom all things exist, in bringing many sons to glory, should make the founder of their salvation perfect through suffering."*

The fundamental aspect of a life in yielded service (servant-hood) to the Lord is humility. In support of that postulation, I'll offer the following portion of Scripture:

> *Have this mind among yourselves, which is yours in Christ Jesus, who, though he was in the form of God, did not count equality with God a thing to be grasped, but emptied himself, by taking the form of a servant, being born in the likeness of men. And being found in human form, he humbled himself by becoming obedient to the point of death, even death on a cross. Therefore, God has highly exalted him and bestowed on him the name that is above every name, so that at the name of Jesus every knee should bow, in heaven and on earth and under the earth, and every tongue confess that Jesus Christ is Lord, to the glory of God the Father.*
>
> ~Philippians 2:5–11

This passage presents the theological concept of *Kenosis:*

Kenosis (from the Greek κένωσις: meaning "emptying") is found primarily in Christian writings, such as the Epistle to the Philippians 2:7, where Jesus is described as having *"...emptied himself..."* (NRSV) to become a servant of humankind. This paradoxical idea of God's "emptying" of Himself to become full of love has intrigued the curiosity of countless theologians, and in the process shaped the development of Christian theology and ethics.

Theologically speaking, Christians have interpreted kenosis as meaning Jesus' sublime humility during the incarnation and complete sacrifice for all, which is simultaneously a call for followers of Christ to be similarly humble and subservient to others.

~New World Encyclopedia,
https://www.newworldencyclopedia.org/entry/Kenosis

We're called to move in obedient service and humility toward God. To be conformed into the image of Christ Jesus, through the sanctifying work of the Holy Ghost, is the charge placed upon all those who purpose to follow the Lord (Rom. 8:29). The Spirit beckons us toward self-emptying, so our lives may reflect the nature and character of our blessed Savior *(Kenosis)*. To be drawn from where we are, to where we're not yet, is the underlying goal ahead of us.

The idea of decreasing, for Christ to increase in us, is a Biblical directive (Jn. 3:30). Knowing Christ in His fullness requires us to die daily, as Scripture says (Phil. 3:10–11). As we approach our futures, the destiny ahead of us and the legacy we pursue impacts what we are purposed to accomplish in seeking the kingdom of God and His righteousness (Mt. 6:33), accepting the highest call as it unfolds before us. The section that follows addresses how we can handle the days that are yet to come.

The Highest Call
~Phil. 3:13–14

The highest call is on my life
Living for Jesus no matter what price
There's a crown of life for those who give their all
Living for Jesus, accepting the highest call

The coming of God's kingdom
As certain as the dawn
Ascends upon a dark and dying land
Lord God, I hear Your calling
By faith I yield my all
And in Your strength, I vow to make my stand
~W. Berry, M. McCall
See & Say Songs, BMI, Circa 1986

Note to reader: A worthwhile read that addresses this subject is *Compassion: A Reflection on the Christian Life* by Nouwen, McNeill, and Morrison (Image Books/Doubleday, 1983).

Destiny and Legacy

A consideration of how Jesus did what He did in Philippians 2:5–11 ushers us directly into our future in terms of calling (destiny) and fulfillment (legacy).

For those whose lives are *"hidden with Christ in God"* (Col. 3:3), their destiny is to take their place *behind* Jesus (Mt. 16:24). Destiny has to do with a calling toward, or a charge upon, one's life. Legacy relates to how we receive (implement and impart) what someone has left behind for us to walk in—or what we leave behind for others to walk in.

> *A person's legacy can become someone else's destiny.*

The term that best describes this dynamic process is *discipleship*—also described as generational transference (see Ps. 78:1–7).

Scripture clearly states that followers of Christ are not their own; they were bought with a price (1 Cor. 6:19, 20). A consecrated lifestyle is offered as a *"living sacrifice,"* (Rom. 12:1). To accomplish that, a believer's life should be understood as being of *"no reputation"* (Phil. 2:5-7, KJV), unnoticed, unannounced, and diminished through humble obedience (1 Pet. 5:6). Lives lived that way are purposed (destined) to travel the same pathway that our Lord did (Phil. 2:8).

The principle of *kenosis* is well expressed in the following verse:

> *"Humble yourselves, therefore, under the mighty hand of God so that at the proper time he may exalt you,"*
> *~1 Pet. 5:6*

It is our job to humble ourselves. It is God's job (according to His will, and His ways) to exalt (lift, elevate) us. If we insist on doing His job, He has no choice but to do ours.

Humble Yourself

~1 Pet. 5:6

VERSE 1:
Humble yourself my brother, in the Presence of the Lord
And wait upon His love to lift you up
Humble yourself my sister, in the Presence of the Lord
And wait upon His love to lift you up

BRIDGE:
A holy life is fashioned through repentance and forgiveness
So humble yourself and He will lift you up
Those who seek to know Him, in reverence bow before Him
And wait upon His love to lift them up

CHORUS:
If you will draw near to God, then He will draw near to you
When you seek to know His will, His mercy cover you
If you will draw near to God, then He will draw near to you
Then as you seek to do His will, His grace will guide you through

VERSE 2:
Humble yourselves, O people, in the Presence of the Lord
And wait upon His love to lift you up
Humble yourselves all nations, in the Presence of the Lord
And wait upon His love to lift you up
~W. Berry, See & Say Songs, BMI

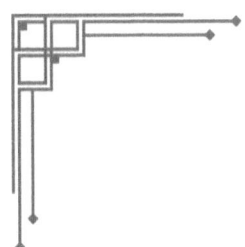

Part Two

Are Y'all Breathin'?

*Let **everything** that hath breath praise the Lord. Praise ye the Lord.*

~Psalm 150:6 KJV, emphasis added

The link between chapter one and chapter two is this:

The commandment stated in Deuteronomy 5:7 is intended for all of humanity. Therefore, the directive of Psalm 150:6 extends to *"everything that has breath."* That means that all living things are capable of, and called to, expressions of worship in some form or fashion. (See Col. 3:17.)

Up to Zion

~Ps. 33:12

CHORUS:
Let's all go up to Zion, let's all go up rejoicing
With tambourines and dancing
With songs and shouts of joy
Mount Zion is God's dwelling place
It's there that we'll behold His face
Let's all go up to Zion
The mountain of the Lord

VERSE ONE:
Praise is in order, for the upright in heart
The heavens awaken, when our praises start
In Him we rejoice, for we trust in His name
His unfailing love rests on all He claims

(Repeat CHORUS)

VERSE TWO:
Every word of the Lord, is faithful and true
And He's bound to accomplish what He said He would do
So let the earth fear the Lord, let the people bow down
And let the universe ring with the joyful sound

(Repeat CHORUS)

CORPORATE READING:
The Lord loves righteousness, the Lord loves justice
The earth is filled with His lovingkindness
Blessed is the nation whose God is the Lord
And the people He has chosen to be His reward
~W. Berry, See & Say Songs, BMI

Let's take a close look at all of Psalm 104. It presents a profound narrative regarding God's sovereign workings in, though, and over all of creation. I encourage you to read it in its entirety and allow the full vista of what it reveals to penetrate your soul. As you do, take note of what it says regarding what takes place with *all* of life, when breath is taken away (v. 29). Then ponder the connection to Psalm 150:6 and see what the Holy Spirit shows you.

Bless the Lord, O my soul! O Lord my God, you are very great! You are clothed with splendor and majesty, covering yourself with light as with a garment, stretching out the heavens like a tent. He lays the beams of his chambers on the waters; he makes the clouds his chariot; he rides on the wings of the wind; he makes his messengers winds, his ministers a flaming fire. He set the earth on its foundations, so that it should never be moved. You covered it with the deep as with a garment; the waters stood above the mountains. At your rebuke they fled; at the sound of your thunder they took to flight. The mountains rose, the valleys sank down to the place that you appointed for them. You set a boundary that they may not pass, so that they might not again cover the earth. You make springs gush forth in the valleys; they flow between the hills; they give drink to every beast of the field; the wild donkeys quench their thirst. Beside them the birds of the heavens dwell; they sing among the branches. From your lofty abode you water the mountains; the earth is satisfied with the fruit of your work. You cause the grass to grow for the livestock and plants for man to cultivate, that he may bring forth food from the earth and wine to gladden the heart of man, oil to make his face shine and bread to strengthen man's heart. The trees of the Lord are watered abundantly, the cedars of Lebanon that he planted. In them the birds build their nests; the stork has her home in the fir trees. The high mountains are for the wild goats; the rocks are a refuge for the rock badgers. He made the moon to mark the seasons; the sun knows its time for setting. You make darkness, and it is night, when all the beasts of the forest creep about. The young lions roar for their prey, seeking their food from God. When the sun rises, they steal away and lie down in their dens. Man goes out to his work and to his labor until the evening. O Lord, how manifold are your works! In wisdom have you made them all; the earth is full of your creatures. Here is the sea, great and wide, which teems with creatures innumerable, living things both small and great. There go the ships, and Leviathan, which you formed to play in it. These all look to you, to give them their food in due season. When you give it to them, they gather it up; when you open your hand, they are filled with good things. When you hide your face, they are dismayed; when you take away their breath, they die and return to their dust. When you send forth your spirit, they are created, and you renew the fact of the ground. **When you hide your face, they are dismayed; when you take away their breath, they die and return to their dust. When you send forth your Spirit, they are created, and you renew the face of the ground.** *May the glory of the Lord endure forever; may the Lord rejoice in his works, who looks on the earth and it trembles, who touches the mountains, and they smoke! I will sing to the Lord as long as I live; I will sing praise to my God while I have being. May my meditation be pleasing to him, for I rejoice in the Lord. Let sinners be consumed from the earth and let the wicked be no more! Bless the Lord, O my soul! Praise the Lord!*

~Psalm 104 emphasis added

The narrative from Spurgeon that follows is so insightful and so beautifully descriptive that I cannot leave it out.

Here we have one of the loftiest and longest sustained flights of the inspired muse. The psalm gives an interpretation to the many voices of nature and sings sweetly both of creation and providence. The poem contains a complete cosmos sea and land, cloud and sunlight, plant and animal, light and darkness, life and death, are all proved to be expressive of the presence of the Lord. Traces of the six days of creation are very evident, and though the creation of man, which was the crowning work of the sixth day, is not mentioned, this is accounted for from the fact that man is himself the singer: some have even discerned marks of the divine resting upon the seventh day in Psalm 104:31. It is a poet's version of Genesis. Nor is it alone the present condition of the earth which is here the subject of song; but a hint is given of those holier times when we shall see "a new earth wherein dwelleth righteousness," out of which the sinner shall be consumed, Psalm 104:35. The spirit of ardent praise to God runs through the whole, and with it a distinct realization of the divine Being as a personal existence, loved and trusted as well as adored.

We have no information as to the author, but the Septuagint assigns it to David, and we see no reason for ascribing it to anyone else. His spirit, style, and manner of writing are very manifest therein, and if the psalm must be ascribed to another, it must be to a mind remarkably similar, and we could only suggest the wise son of David—Solomon, the poet preacher, to whose notes upon natural history in the Proverbs. Some of the verses bear a striking likeness. Whoever the human penman may have been, the exceeding glory and perfection of the Holy Spirit's own divine authorship are plain to every spiritual mind."

~Charles Spurgeon, *The Treasury of David*
Thomas Nelson, 1997 Originally published in 1885

Most High God
~Ps. 104

With all authority, splendor and majesty
You are the Most High God
Adorned with beams of light, across the heavens bright
You are the Most High God

The winds obey Your will, when You speak, "Peace be still"
You are the Most High God
The holy fire fall, is Yours alone to call
You are the Most High God

CHORUS:
Most High, Most High
You are the Most High God
(Repeat)

Over the waters deep, above each mountain peak
You are the Most High God
All of creation sings, proclaiming you as King
You are the Most High God

The sun and moon above, reflect Your boundless love
You are the Most High God
The wonders of Your hand, reveal Your "Master Plan"
You are the Most High God

(Repeat CHORUS)

All nature bows to You, as it was made to do
You are the Most High God
Your glory will endure, throughout the ages sure

You are the Most High God
(Repeat CHORUS)

~W. Berry, See & Say Songs, BMI

God's providential rule, carried out through his Sovereign reign, sustains all living things through His divine will. And the gift of life—its essence—is established, sustained, and resolved directly through the breath of life that only the Creator can impart, or withdraw.

> Everything depends upon the breath of God. When God gives it, life on earth is sustained. When God withholds it, trees die, rivers dry up, birds vanish. The whole of creation prays *"...take not your wind from us,"* for by it we live (see Ps. 5:11).
> ~Walter Bruggemann, *Texts Under Negotiation*
> Fortress Press, 1993

Brueggemann is a noted Old Testament scholar and theologian. The working knowledge he carries has impacted me (and countless others) for decades. The Holy Ghost brought the above quote across my path as I've been developing this material.

Rather than use the word *Spirit* as the King James Version does, he uses the word *wind*. In doing so, the wind is describing the breath of the Spirit. As I read his usage, it appears that *wind, Spirit,* and *breath* are synonymous. I say that because in this text, the Hebrew word for *Spirit* is *Ruwach*, meaning wind (by resemblance, breath, exhalation).

The very breath of God initiated life in Adam. That is to say that the sustaining power of life itself was/is a direct result of that Divine action. From that act, all of humankind was born.

> *"God formed Man out of dirt from the ground and blew into his nostrils the breath of life. The Man came alive—a living soul!"*
> ~Gen.2:7 MSG

This relinks me to a personal experience I had some twenty

years ago. Consider the following narrative as it relates to one of the *whys* of worship.

Worship on the Wind (A Personal Revelation)

> *Blowing toward the south, then turning toward the north, the wind continues swirling along; and on its circular courses the wind returns.*
> ~Ecclesiastes 1:6

In September of 2004, during my first sojourn to the continent of Africa, this happened: The story concerns an event that deeply impacted my life, my perceptions about living, and my future/destiny. In fact, the term "life-changing" is appropriate for what I now share.

The story begins in late September of 2004, standing in the middle of nowhere in Kenya, Africa. I was returning with a short-term mission team from a region located in the very shadow of Mt. Kilimanjaro.

We had spent ten days or so building two church structures for the Maasai tribespeople who had converted to Christianity. After finishing and dedicating (consecrating) both buildings, we started our journey out of the "bush" toward a paved highway that would take us back to Nairobi.

Driving along roads that really weren't roads at all, one of our Land Rovers broke down. Fortunately, our team guide had the know-how and the tools needed to make the necessary repairs. However, doing so was going to take a while. So, we all piled out of our vehicles and purposed to make the most of our time until things got sorted out.

Note: Waiting patiently for circumstances to change is a major part of the African lifestyle. It's in the DNA of those on the continent. (If you go there, you will find that out for yourself.)

Here's what happened:

During our time together as a team, we had learned that we weren't to walk too far away from the others when we were out in the "bush." Things could get dangerous in such an environment. So, staying within eyesight of each other was important. Our team leader had released us to roam the area near the vehicles, instructing us to stay close. We began to amble around in groups of twos and threes, while a few of us went off individually a brief distance away. I had walked away by myself to take care of nature's call behind a couple of scrub trees, when something very unusual began to occur.

As I turned to head back, facing into the breeze that was rising out of the valley just below us, I began to hear what sounded like music. More specifically, it sounded like singing. To be exact, it sounded like children singing. And to fine tune that even further, I heard children singing what seemed to me like worship. The "sound" was very brief—two or three seconds at the most. But I know worship when I hear it. It's a *deep calls to deep* kind of thing (Ps. 42:7).

What I heard stunned me. How could this be happening? We were in "the middle of nowhere," so how could there be singing? Where would it come from? And how could it be kids' voices?

As I continued to turn my face directly toward the wind, the sound disappeared. As soon as it was there, it was gone. I stopped in my tracks and began to try and figure out what was taking place. I turned my head ever so slightly to re-center myself, and when I did, the wind shifted and blew more directly into my ear instead of straight into my face. When that happened, the sound returned. This time it was as clear as a bell, but not very loud. (Got the picture?)

So, at this point, I was getting excited because my brain and my senses were starting to catch up with my spirit. I turned my face directly back into the wind and again the sound disappeared. Now I was onto something that was beyond my immediate comprehension. I tried it once more, turning my head away from the wind blowing at me directly, allowing the air current to blow into my ear instead of my face.

Just then, what was happening hit me light a bolt of lightning: What I was hearing was on the wind—or *in* the wind. The sound was coming from somewhere I had yet to determine, and it was being carried on/by the wind itself. In fact, it couldn't be detected unless my ear was turned exactly the right way to catch the sound as it blew in my direction. In other words—*without being positioned properly, I couldn't hear the singing at all.*

Saints, that'll preach!

I glanced back up the ridge to see if any of the other team members knew what I was experiencing. Not a clue—they had heard nothing. They weren't positioned (tuned in) to it at all.

I was having a divine appointment, and people within earshot of me had no idea!

Selah (Pause & ponder.)

Once I realized what kind of "moment" I was in, I locked into the sound like a laser-tracking-beam. I began to move toward it, but every time I turned directly into the wind, I lost the singing. I could only stay on track by turning my head ever-so-slightly every few steps. That way, the wind carried the sound into my ear, and I could adjust my path of pursuit accordingly.

My heart was pounding, my soul caught up in the dynamics of what was taking place. I had to know where the singing was coming from, and who was creating it. So, up toward the top of the ridge, I ran yelling like a crazy man for the others to join me—but there was a problem. The angle I was moving in was taking me away from my team, and the wind was carrying the sound of my voice (along with the sound of the singing) away from my comrades.

The only person near enough to really hear me was Patti,

a sister from our worship choir back in our home church. As I motioned for her to meet me at the top of the ridge, she began to head in that direction.

She had no idea what was waiting up at the crest—and neither did I.

As Patti and I topped the rise of the ridge, we saw the valley opening below and beyond us, toward a small mountain range in the distance. The valley wasn't very deep, but it was wide and long. As we looked down over the edge, we could see a dry riverbed, which continued out and away from where we stood. At the base of the ridge just below us, we saw something besides land and space. There appeared to be a sort of fort made from slender tree trunks which had been stripped clean of their bark. The fort was constructed in a rectangular shape, four walls of wood with no ceiling, open to the sky.

As we stood there trying to figure out what we were seeing, everything suddenly locked into place in one profoundly amazing moment. The wind off the valley floor picked up and began to rise, wafting up the side of the ridge to where we were positioned looking downward. And what it carried up to us was now hitting us square in our faces.

It was the sound of children singing at the top of their voices.

It was a precious and passionate sound. Such beauty and wonder in a dry and barren place. This "no place" in "the middle of nowhere" had become a high and holy place. I turned toward Patti who, up until that moment, had no idea of why I had called her to join me there. She hadn't heard a sound—till it rose up on the wind and overwhelmed her.

I looked at her with tears in my eyes (matched by her own) and said, "Patti, it's a school, and the kids are singing praise songs!"

There, under the open and expansive African sky, the Holy Ghost fell big time, and my sister and I were overcome by the sound, tears, smiles, and joy of it all.

In the very next instant, one side of the "fort" where a doorway was positioned opened up, and all the kids ran out of their classroom, made a turn, and flowed into the dry riverbed, laughing, jumping, and having a grand time of it. I looked at Patti through more tears and said, "It's recess." We both began to laugh out loud as we thanked God for His precious gift to us.

As we stood there taking it all in, the Holy Ghost spoke to me with a word of revelation. He said, "No place, is some place, to somebody."

At that moment, my global perspective exploded. My view of humanity, the nations, and God's ever-expanding kingdom, took on entirely new dimensions. My understanding of His Omnipresence had been blown totally off the charts. I was awestruck!

This gift, this divine appointment, continues to impact my life and ministry almost daily. As I reflect on it once again, I'll say this: God's "otherness" is a very real thing to encounter. The eternal dynamics of His kingdom—the ebb and flow—are constantly at work. We are *compassed about* (Ps. 32:7, KJV) by the sights and sounds of His Divine Presence in truly supernatural ways.

Allow the Spirit of the Lord to open up your senses, your soul and your very being to the glory and wonder of it all.

And may His kingdom come (manifest) on earth as it is in heaven.

Let me mention one last thing to those of you who lead congregations in corporate worship on a regular basis. Please be encouraged by this *fact!* Worship—heart-felt, soul-engaged, pure, honest and undefiled worship—is being released all over this earth every moment of every day (24/7/365). God has purposed and ordained it to be this way (see Ps.150:6 and Luke 19:40). But the thing is, we're not always standing in the right spot, at the right moment, with our heads turned just the right way to be able to hear it. Nonetheless, it is there. I can personally testify to the fact that there is worship on the wind, coming from people in places that you'd never imagine.

All of heaven's waiting
All the earth expecting
Sons, daughters, arise
Singing songs of freedom
Words of healing
One voice, wind-blown worship
~Denise Graves, "Hallelujah." ©Denise Graves

For worship to be on the wind (airborne), it was first born from inside of the children described in the narrative I've just related. Beginning as a stirring from deep within their hearts, the breath of life filled their lungs. Thereafter, it was exhaled through their mouths as worship, and the sound of praise rose up into the air. From there, the wind carried it wherever the breezes chose to send it. That process is supported Scripturally in John 3:8 saying, *"The wind blows where it wishes, and you hear its sound, but you do not know where it comes from or where it goes. So it is with everyone who is born of the Spirit."*

Reconsidering Worship

In pondering worship, the topic of praise inevitably comes up. It's important to take note of the similarities and distinctions of both concepts.

Three Axioms:

1. We worship God with our praises, and we praise God when we worship.
2. Worship is obedient service, manifesting through self-sacrifice.
3. Praise is the celebrative response to the Father, Son, and Holy Ghost.

Worship is the process by which the principles and precepts of God's kingdom are worked into, and out of, the lives of believers in intimate relationship with the Father, Son, and Holy Ghost, through faithful obedience, sacrificial service, and personal and corporate offerings of adoration and exaltation.

Worship is a noun *or* a verb, depending on how it is communicated. It's a noun because it has form and substance—it is a thing. It is also a verb because it is something we do—requiring action (or better yet, engagement). According to Romans 12:1, it can be Biblically understood as being part of everything we do (see the Message Bible).

Praise is the celebrative response to the God of the kingdom, Christ Jesus (our blessed Savior), and the indwelling person of the Holy Spirit. If you'd like a Scriptural basis for what I've said, try this one:

> *"Let every detail in your lives—words, actions, whatever—be done in the name of the Master, Jesus, thanking God the Father every step of the way,"*
>
> ~Col. 3:17, MSG

Distinct, Not Separate

Worship and Praise are distinct, not separate. They are like two sides of the same coin, so to speak. Let me develop that thought for you:

From *Webster's Dictionary:*

Separate: Solitary; set or kept apart; detached; not shared with another; individual.

Distinct: Distinguishable; things similar in effect by wholly in motive; presenting a clear unmistakable impression.

The contemporary church today understands (or misunderstands) worship and praise as two separate things. To make matters worse theologically, the current perception of each is that praise is offered up in our congregational gatherings using up-beat, up-tempo songs—most often sung in the early portion of our services. Worship, on the other hand, presumably takes place among

35

us when we are singing slower (and more emotionally sensitive) songs—sung closer to or just before the sermon takes place. Allow me just one brief moment to vent here: That is simply nonsense!

The first problem with that theological approach is that we are limiting both actions (praise and worship) to subjective expressions confined to personal experiences in the context of corporate gatherings. By doing so we compartmentalize them. Such expressed experiences are most certainly Biblical in their outworking. But they are only components of a much larger concept. They are not the concept in total. To be Scriptural, worship and praise should be considered (and integrated) into our lives and lifestyles together, not relegated to specific times in specific locations. The place, time, or circumstance isn't the point. The focus of our praise and worship is.

> "Jesus said to her, 'Woman, believe Me, an hour is coming when neither in this mountain nor in Jerusalem will you worship the Father,'"
>
> ~Jn. 4:21

The next problem—as I see it—is that by separating the two components, we uncouple them, when in fact they are not intended to be such. Here's why: When they are separated, over time they become aspects of our lives which cannot, and do not, take place together. They become sectioned off and categorized. Whereas, if they are perceived as being distinct (which is what they really are), then the interchange between them offers us the opportunity to experience and express them in a seamless flow of celebration, adoration, exaltation, awe, and reverence.

Pastor Timothy Keller's comments provide a perspective of this idea of distinct instead of separate. Writing about Psalm 95:1–4, he says:

> This psalm and the next give us almost liturgy for a service of gathered worship. The first stage is adoration.

Let us rise up in joy to God the Creator (vs.1–5). Let us praise Him for being the maker and sustainer of the world. *Worshipping is not always quiet and decorous. It can entail shouting, praising, leaping to our feet, singing out hearts out.* When the love of the immeasurably great and transcendent God of the universe becomes real to us, the joy should be uncontainable.

~Tim Keller, *The Songs of Jesus*
Viking Books, 2015, emphasis added

Then continuing his insights with verses five through seven, he states:

The next element of worship is confession of our sin and need. Let us bow down in humility to God the Redeemer (vs. 6–7). In contrast to the exuberance of the first five verses, which fits with the postures of standing or even dancing, each of the three verbs in verse 6 have to do with getting low before God, since the Hebrew word for worship here literally means to prostrate one-self. We are to bow reverently, to kneel humbly before God, admitting our sinfulness and dependence. While adoration comes from seeing a God of glory, submission comes from seeing a God of grace, one who is our covenant God, who redeemed us and brought us as sheep into His fold (verse 7).

~Keller, *The Songs of Jesus*

Here you can clearly see that the components of praise and worship are interchangeable. As they both take place within the same psalm, their outworking flows naturally from the heart of the Psalmist (see Heb. 4:7) with no thought given to any aspects of what we now consider necessary to "enter in" to a "worship experience."

In *The Treasury of David*, Charles Spurgeon says of this same Psalm:

> This is a Psalm of *invitation to worship*. It has a ring like church bells, and like the bells, it sounds both *merry and solemn*. At first it rings out a lively peal, and then it drops to a funeral kneel, as if tolling at the funeral of the generation that perished in the wilderness. We will call it, "The Psalm of the Provocation."
> ~Spurgeon, *The Treasury of David*, emphasis added

Spurgeon goes on to say of verse one, "Let us sing with holy enthusiasm and make a sound that shows our earnestness. Let us lift our voices with abounding joy, actuated by that happy and peaceful spirit that trusting love is sure to foster." Then continuing, his commentary of verse two is, "We may come boldly into the immediate presence of the Lord, for the Holy Spirit's voice in this Psalm invites us, but when we draw near, we should remember His great goodness and cheerfully confess it." (Spurgeon, *The Treasury of David*.)

Such insights as these help to shed light on just how unified both aspects of adoration are Biblically distinct, not separate. Worship and praise are not divided between fast songs—at the beginning of our corporate services, and slow songs (setting an atmosphere for the sermon of the day). They belong together, like two sides of the same coin.

Our worship isn't segregated internally, as we currently understand and practice it. It is integrated (deep within our souls) and includes each Scriptural example that we can incorporate into our sacrificial offerings, both personally and corporately.

Our Father does not seek worship; He seeks worshippers. Worship is not merely something we do in meetings. It is a lifestyle, or it simply is not worship. Worship is a spontaneous response to the presence of God. If we would live our lives in awareness of the presence of God we would always be worshipping. In corporate worship, worshippers gather to encourage one another and express their appreciation together. They are not enjoying worship; they are enjoying Father.

~Fount Lee Shults, Facebook, Brother Fount Page, "Morning Meditation," August 10, 2016

The best example I've found in the Scriptures of worship manifesting in a worshipper's life is:

Because Your lovingkindness is better than life, my lips will praise (shabach—to shout) You. So I will bless (barak— to bow in adoration) You as long as I live; I will lift up my hands (towah—to extend the hands in surrender) in Your name. My soul is satisfied as with marrow and fatness, and my mouth offers praises (halal—to jump for joy; to rave for God; to go wild with celebration) with joyful lips. When I remember You on my bed, I meditate on You in the night watches, for You have been my help, and in the shadow of Your wings I sing for joy (rana—to shout with abandon).
Psalm 63:3–7 NASB, Hebrew insertions added

The dynamic expressions above are taking place as one overflowing sacrifice of emotion(s): moving back and forth, and in and out of several praise and worship components and postures, all at the same time. What a beautifully incorporated view we are given here of a worshipper's intimate relationship of self-expression(s) to the Father, Son, and Holy Ghost. Would that we adapt this example as our own—both personally and congregationally.

"A worshipper is one who is intimately acquainted with and has a daily relationship with God exhibited

through obedience."
~John W. Stevenson, *Worshipper by Design*
Xulon Press, 2009

If it is our intention to live as *"true worshippers" (Jn. 4:24)*, then our worship is to be Trinitarian in nature and substance. We are called (commanded) to worship God the Father, Son, and Holy Ghost—the Three in One. According to Scripture, and validated in church history, our *"service of worship" (Rom. 12:1, NASB)* isn't to be offered separately to the three distinct persons of the Trinity. Rather, it is to be inclusive—unified, if you will—in terms of Who our worship is focused on, directed toward, and exalting of.

This view has been celebrated since the third century, as demonstrated in the writings of Polycarp:

"The God we worship is Trinitarian in nature—Father, Son and Holy Spirit—co-equal and, therefore, each worthy of worship.

"Wherefore also I praise you [God, the Father] for all things, I bless you, along with the everlasting and heavenly Jesus Christ, your beloved Son, with whom, to you and the Holy Spirit, be glory both now and to all coming ages. Amen."
~Epistle from Smyrna, XIV

Praise God from Whom all blessings flow
Praise Him all creatures here below
Praise Him above, ye heavenly hosts
Praise Father, Son, and Holy Ghost
~Thomas Ken, "The Doxology." 17th Century

We keep messin' up how we understand and apply ourselves to the entire subject of worship by holding on to, and continuing to, repeat two basic theological misconceptions:

1. Worship and praise are not separate things. They are distinct. Separating them not only weakens their kingdom witness to the world-at-large, it also diminishes their impact on us personally in relationship to our sacrificial offerings.
2. Worship is not solely to be understood as having to do with music, songs, singing, and emotionally experienced expressions taking place in congregational gatherings. It isn't about location. It is about internal engagement (see Ps. 35:9–10a).

The longer we continue to allow those two misconceptions to define our theological perceptions of worship, the further away we'll move (wander) from a Biblically based understanding of what it is intended to be. Whereas emotion, experience, dynamic expressions (personally and corporately) should be considered as part of our worship offering, they are only aspects of it. They are not the total substance of worship itself.

Our understanding will never be truly Biblical without a building up from the basic meaning of what worship is to be from a Scriptural viewpoint.

The Principle of First Mention

There is a principle that is taught and often used in the study of the Bible called the principle of first usage. Basically, how it is to be applied is that the first time a word (or subject) is presented in Scripture, it should become the default setting from which all other usages are drawn from. When you apply that principle to *worship,* the starting place becomes Genesis 22:5. That's where Abraham speaks to his servants, telling them that he and Isaac will, *"go over there; and we will worship and return to you," (NASB).* That's where worship is first mentioned in the Bible.

In Jewish history, this scene is considered second in importance to the deliverance that took place at the crossing of the Red Sea. Its prominence in their religion (and in their congregational gatherings) is a touchstone of faith in action. It's an "Ebenezer" of sorts (a place of remembrance). But here's the interesting and troubling thing about this story. It is a scene in which we are shown a father being commanded to effectively execute his only son as an act of sacrificial obedience. An act that Scripture tells us Abraham understood as being one of worship. There is just no way our temporal minds can embrace such a scenario without becoming totally confused and completely undone. It is simply beyond our understanding.

Eugene Peterson's comments on this event are insightful and well worth considering:

> The defining event in the way of Abraham takes place on Mount Moriah: The Binding of Isaac, the Akedah (the term the rabbis use for this story, after the Hebrew word for "binding"). Abraham binding Isaac and offering him as a sacrifice on the altar that he has just built expressly for the purpose. This story has absorbed the imagination of the people of God and plunged generation after generation of us into facing and dealing with the fundamental mystery that is God: There is so much here that we cannot comprehend, so much that violates our pious sensibilities, so much that refuses to conform to our expectations. How can God command a murder? And not just murder in general but the murder of a beloved son? How can God go back on the miracle-promise fulfilled in the birth of Isaac? How can God, who our parents and pastors have taught us loves us from eternity, command this cold-blooded cruelty? How can God, who Jesus tells us has such a tender heart that he is moved even by the death of sparrows, command a father to kill his son, without so much as a hint of explanation?
>
> ~Peterson, *The Jesus Way*
> Wm. B. Eerdman's Publishing, 2007

I would add: How, in the process of carrying out such a difficult command, can Abraham call it worship?

From where we stand, on the other side of this Biblically-historical story, how can we even begin to reach a place where our so called "contemporary worship" comes anywhere near embracing the depth of self-sacrifice and faithful obedience that we see in a scene such as this—and then call it worship? Yet, this story is where we find the first reference to worship taking place. It is where the Biblical foundation of worship has been laid. It is here that we are provided a base on which to build. Regardless of how mysterious this may appear to us; it is nonetheless the starting point for how worship is to be approached and appropriated theologically. My personal perspective about all this is that we need to reboot our perception of what worship means, and then rebuild from there.

Note to reader: You might want to consider doing a Google search of "the binding" *(Akedah)* to gain a little more insight on the subject.

In the Beginning

The first person of humankind (Adam) was given breath directly from Jehovah God (Gen. 2:7). Centuries later, the impartation of the Holy Ghost took place when Jesus did exactly what the Father had done when His breath filled Adams lungs:

> *"Jesus said to them again, 'Peace be with you. As the Father has sent me, even so I am sending you.' And when he had said this, he breathed on them and said to them, 'Receive the Holy Spirit,'"*
>
> ~Jn. 20:21–22

Scripture begins by stating that *"God created the heavens and the earth…" (Gen. 1:1).* Then, in verse three, it goes on to say how that took place: *"Then God said…"*

43

Following the unfolding of the creation story, Genesis 2:7 says, *"Then the Lord God formed man of dust from the ground, and beathed into his nostrils the breath of life; and man became a living being."* As I've highlighted earlier in Psalm 104:29, the narrative declares that life itself is given and sustained by the breath of God. Biblically speaking, that gives us five distinct aspects for consideration:

1. God is Creator
2. God speaks
3. God breathes
4. Humankind was created by God
5. God gives and sustains *all* life

The extension of this continues in the New Testament saying, *"All scripture is God-breathed..." (2 Tim. 3:16a)*. From this standpoint, we see the following:

Creation of heaven and earth took place through God's speaking, which was energized and discharged by His breath. We also see that life itself is given and sustained by His breath (Ps. 104:29). And that *"All Scripture"* was inspired (imparted, given) by and through the breath of God (2 Tim. 2:16). When you factor in all the categories of life on earth—based on the exposition in Psalm 104—it is apparent that breath (breathing) is the very essence of life itself.

The process of harmonization between breath, wind, and worship is implied in the verse that opened this chapter. The directive given in Psalm 150:6b is more than a suggestion for consideration, it is a Biblical command.

The Breath of Life

As I was finishing this chapter, as happenstance would have it, I found myself in what seemed to be a random conversation with a dear Kingdom comrade. I've been in a relationship with Pastor Barbie for over thirty years of friendship and ministry. When I mentioned the focus of this chapter, she began to share a teaching she'd fashioned some years back:

One important thing to understand is that true blessings (especially in the Old Testament) came through the fathers, and were given out of all that he had regarding *possession, wisdom and power...* All throughout the Word you will find examples of the blessing passed from generation to generation through the words of the fathers. In fact, there had to be a *pronouncement* of the blessing in order for it to actually be put into effect, and once in effect, it could not be revoked. This is why Esau grieved so deeply, knowing the words had been said over his brother, and could not be taken back. *Selah.* Still, until the blessing *rode breath*, it was merely a *thought*, a wish, or perhaps even a promise. But when the blessing was breathed... ah, life was released!

Knowing this, I find great insight regarding the breath blessing in the following passage of scripture:

"Praise be to the God and Father of our Lord Jesus Christ, who has blessed us in the heavenly realms with every spiritual blessing in Christ..." (Eph. 1:3).

It literally defines out as...

Eulogeo—pronounce

Epouraneous—from the place of God and angels

Pneumotikos—breath

Eulogia—blessing

This means the *Ruach* (the breath of God blessing) is an *invocation* of benefits given from the place of God and angels. It is the breath that speaks the final words of consecrated purpose; the breath that flows from the place of God and angels and declares the benefit, invoking—calling forth and putting into effect—the favor and blessing of God. So, why would we ever stop praying, *Ruach*, breath of God, breathe over us...?

Ruah

Oh, how we need, oh, how we long
Oh, how our hearts pant for You

So, now we weep
So, now we grown
So, now our spirits cry for You
Let our tears become prayers
Our prayers become incense
Let this incense lift to You, our hearts desire

Ruah, breathe over us
Ruah, breathe over us
Ruah, breathe over us
Breath of God

© Barbie Loflin, used by permission

Note to reader: A follow-up narrative for this chapter may be found in chapter six of Walter Brueggemann's book, *Our Hearts Wait* (Westminster John Knox Press, 2022). Also, chapter sixteen of John Piper's book, *Provision* (Crossways Publishing, 2020).

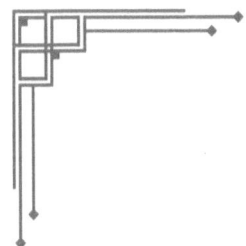

Part Three

A CONGREGATIONAL RESPONSE

But thou art holy, O thou that inhabitest the praises of Israel.

~Psalm 22:3 KJV

Without breath, there is no life. Without life, there is no active worship possible.

No one in the world of the dead can thank you or praise you; none of those in the deep pit can hope for you to show them how faithful you are. Only the living can thank you, as I am doing today. Each generation tells the next about your faithfulness.

~Isaiah 38:18–19 CEV

Being that breath is required for worship to manifest, such a God-given gifting applies not only to individuals, but also to groupings of worshippers. The progression from the previous chapters links directly to the narrative postulations expressed in this chapter.

Why Do We Sing in Church?

The key word for consideration in the verse above is *inhabitest*. Effectively, it means to sit down. However, a more expansively-detailed definition will help to develop my theses. Strong's Bible Concordance provides a basic explanation from the Hebrew language:

Inhabitest *(Yashab)*—To sit down (as a judge); to dwell with or among; to remain; to settle, to marry. To abide or continue. To inhabit a place; to keep house; to return to or be seated. To tarry; to establish a habitation.

To begin unpacking that concept, I'll mention that *inhabitest* only appears once in Scripture. That's in verse three of Psalm 22. However, the word *seat* is used many times. And often when it is, it conveys the same (or similar) meaning as *inhabitest*. They can be considered as stating the same intention whenever the Hebrew word *Yashab* is intended or implied.

I'll use a passage from Job to explain what I believe is taking place when God *shows up* to join His people during corporate/congregational singing.

Read Job 29, and note verse seven which says:

> *"When I went out to the gate through the city, when I prepared my seat in the street."*
>
> ~Job 29:7 KJV

According to Strong's, in Hebrew the word *seat* is *mo-shab*, meaning a site or session, by extension an abode (in place or time); to populate, assemble, dwell in.

Clearly, much of what's expressed in the Hebrew language for *seat* is compatible with the Hebrew word for *inhabitest*. There is a linked relationship between both images. Therefore, there is a similarity between Job being seated at the gate (Job 29:7), and God (Jehovah) being seated upon the praises of His people (Ps. 22:3). At least, there appears to be as I see it.

Considering what happened when Job took his position of authority, a vista is provided into what happens when God does the same thing by being *present on purpose*. This is what Scripture tells us regarding the dynamics presented in Job 29:

> *And Job again took up his discourse, and said: "Oh, that I were as in the months of old, as in the days when God watched over me, when his lamp shone upon my head, and by his light I walked through darkness, as I was in my prime, when the friendship of God was upon my tent, when the Almighty was yet with me, when my children were all around me, when my steps were washed with butter, and the rock poured out for me streams of oil! When I went out to the gate of the city, when I prepared my seat in the square the young men saw me and withdrew, and the aged rose and stood; the princes refrained from talking and laid their hand on their mouth; the voice of the nobles was hushed, and their tongue stuck to the roof of their mouth. When the ear heard, it called me blessed, and when the eye saw, it approved, because I delivered the poor who cried for help, and the fatherless who had none to help him.*
>
> *The blessing of him who was about to perish came upon me, and I caused the widow's heart to sing for joy. I put on righteousness, and it clothed me; my justice was like a robe and a turban. I was eyes to the blind and feet to the lame. I was a father to the needy, and I searched out the cause of him whom I did not know. I broke the fangs of the unrighteous and made him drop his prey from his teeth. Then I thought, "I shall die in my nest, and I shall multiply my days as the sand, my roots spread out to the waters, with the dew all night on my branches, my glory fresh with me, and my bow ever new in my hand." Men listened to me and waited and kept silence for my counsel. After I spoke they did not speak again, and my word dropped upon them.*

They waited for me as for the rain, and they opened their mouths as for the spring rain. I smiled on them when they had no confidence, and the light of my face they did not cast down. I chose their way and sat as chief, and I lived like a king among his troops, like one who comforts mourners.

Verses one through six tell us how Job remembers once being favored by the Lord, and how he felt about being so profoundly blessed. In verse seven, he goes on to reflect on how his position of sitting at the gate, of being favored and blessed with authority, impacted those in the community.

Now, moving forward to verse twenty-five, note that the word *sat* is the same word as *inhabitest* in Psalm 22:3. It speaks of enthronement. The Hebrew word in both passages is *Yashab*, conveying the exact same meaning in each verse. That's how Job perceived his role of authority. I pose that this is the very same role that God functions in when He takes His place on the throne His people build for Him, constructed out of their corporate songs of praise, adoration, and exaltation.

Being seated at the gate is historically rooted in the tradition of how elder leadership functioned in Old Testament times, and how the people responded to them:

> "Gates in Biblical Israel weren't just a doorway into the city. They were where prophets cried out and kings judged, and people met..."
>
> ~Rogoff, Mike
> "When King David Sat 'In the Gate,' What Did That Mean?"
> https://www.haaretz.com/archaeology/2015-02-24/
> ty-article/.premium/gates-in-the-bible-not-what-you-
> thought/0000017f-e586-dea7-adff-f5ffa4fd0000

To me, this unfolding narrative links so clearly to Psalm 22:7, which anchors this concept:

Besides being part of a city's protection against invaders, city gates were places of central activity in Biblical times. It was at the city gates that important business transactions were made, court was convened, and public announcements were heralded. Accordingly, it is natural that the Bible frequently speaks of "sitting in the gate" or of the activities that took place at the gate. In Proverbs 1, wisdom is personified: *"At the head of the noisy streets she cries out, in the gateways of the city she makes her speech"* (v.21). To spread her words to the maximum number of people, Wisdom took to the gates.

~https://www.gotquestions.org/city-gate.html.

We see Jesus, His disciples, and multitudes of people in a similar dynamic scene as presented in Job 29. Considering Job 29 and Matthew 5:1–2 together can serve to focus and reinforce what's stated in Psalm 22:3.

> *"Seeing the crowds, he went up on the mountain, and when he sat down, his disciples came to him,"*
> ~Matthew 5:1–2

It appears (to me) that our contemporary perspective regarding the Presence of God in our so-called "worship services" is often predicated on either our feelings related to Him being there, or our emotions related to what we expect to happen if/when He does [in fact] show up. Such feelings and emotions may be honest, heart-felt, and authentic in terms of our motives and expectations. But Psalm 139:7–12 clearly states that God is [in fact] everywhere, all the time. That is what Omnipresence is—that's what it means. And, for those who consider themselves to be followers of Christ, reconciled (2 Cor. 5:17–21), redeemed, and *"hidden with Christ in God" (Col. 3:1–4),* 1 Corinthians 3:16 makes it clear that His abiding Presence is housed inside of us.

Based on the context and content of Job 29, the Biblical dynamic seems to be this in essence:

God's people built Him a throne out of their corporate *praises. The size of the throne is based on the size of the praise being offered up.

*Little praise, little throne, big praise, big throne, extra-large praise, etc.

> Praise is a liturgical act with its own "reasons of the heart," not submitted to the reasons of this age...it is our fleeting resolve to have done with technique and control as ways of locating sense, meaning, value, and hope in our lives. Liturgy is embrace of an alternative image of reality.
> ~Walter Brueggemann, *Our Hearts Wait*, Westminster Knox, 2022

The Importance of Continuous Massive Praise

In 1980, during my time of study and spiritual formation at Elim Bible Institute (Elim, New York), another student handed me a little book entitled *Destined For The Throne* by Paul E. Billheimer. Although much of what it addressed was beyond me spiritually at the time, it has turned out to be a source of inspiration and direction for over forty years. The section that follows here is quoted directly from it. The insights it contains have kept it in print since it was first published in 1975.

> To be most effective, then, praise must be massive, continuous, a fixed habit, a full-time occupation, a diligently pursued vocation, a total way of life.... [T]he praise which overcomes is not merely occasional or spasmodic praise, praise that fluctuates with moods and circumstances. It is continuous praise, praise that is a

vocation, a way of life. "I will bless (praise) the Lord at all times; His praise shall continually be in my mouth" (Ps. 34:1). "Blessed are those that dwell in thy house; they will be still (always) praising thee" (Ps. 84:4). It has been pointed out that in heaven praise is so important that it constitutes the total occupation of a certain order of beings (Rev. 4:8). God gave David such a revelation of the importance and power of praise upon earth that following the heavenly pattern, He set aside and dedicated an army of four thousand Levites whose sole occupation was to praise the Lord (1 Chron. 23:5). They did nothing else. One of the last official acts of King David before his death was the organization of a formal program of praise. Each morning and each evening a contingent of these four thousand Levites engage in this service, "And to stand every evening" (1 Chron. 23:30). To the shame and defeat of the Church, the significance of the massive praise content of the word has been largely overlooked."

~Paul E. Billheimer, *Destined for the Throne*
Bethany House, 1983

Brueggemann echoes Billheimer's assertion when he states,

"My urging is a modest one: that serious parishes and congregations must invest greatly and intentionally as communities of praise, and, indeed, that they have no more important work to do."

~Brueggemann, *Our Hearts Wait*
Westminster Knox, 2022

Praise Is Where God Lives

There are two unifying reasons *why* our corporate worship is joined together in this chapter. One is that God's supernatural "otherness" is present when His people gather in praise and worship—that's His inhabiting—His dwelling in/among/with us. The other is that our response-ability to make space for Him to do what He does is essential for multiple aspects of His Sovereign will to be imparted in our congregational gatherings—that's His enthronement.

> *Behold how good and pleasant it is when believers dwell in unity! It is like the precious oil on the head, running down on the beard, on the beard of Aaron, running down on the collar of his robes! It is like the dew of Hermon, which falls on the mountains of Zion! For there the Lord has commanded the blessing, life forevermore.*
> ~Psalm 133:1–3

Unity

~Ps. 133

Behold how good and pleasant it is
When believers are gathered in unity
It's like the dew of Hermon
Coming down on Mt. Zion
When the people of God see their destiny

For there the Lord commands a blessing
When He hears us all rejoicing
In the bond that's been created
Through the blood of our Redeemer

(He gives us) life forevermore
He gives us life forevermore
He gives us life forevermore
When we are united in Him

Behold how good and pleasant it is
To be seated with God in the heavenlies
It's like the dew of Hermon
Coming down on Mt. Zion
And washing away our iniquity

~W. Berry, See & Say Songs, BMI

In Ps. 22:3 we read, "Yet you are enthroned as the Holy One; you are the praise of Israel." The King James says it more distinctly, "But thou art holy, O thou that inhabitest the praises of Israel." In other words, praise is where God lives. It is his permanent address. Praise is his home element. He is at home in praise. He is "great and greatly to be praised" (Ps. 48:11).

This settles one of the vast mysteries which accompanies praise. Why is it that when we praise the Lord things change so rapidly? Why does healing come on wings of praise? Why do human emotions undergo such a transition when praise is the choice? How are we to account for those things which accompany praise? The simple answer is: While God is everywhere present, he is not everywhere manifested. He is at home in praise and, being at home, he manifests himself best as God! When you or I choose to make go a home through praise, we invite him to act "at home." When God is "at home" in praise he does what he wants to do.

~Jack Taylor, *The Hallelujah Factor*
Broadman Press, 1983

The word *praises* in Psalm 22:3 is *tehillah*. In Hebrew it means laudation, a hymn. Usually corporate/congregational in nature. From the root word *halal*, meaning to shine, to make a show, to boast; to be clamorously foolish. To rave or go wild for God (Strong's Bible Concordance).

All that has to do with the glory *(Kabod)*, the heavy of God's manifesting Presence (see 2 Chron. 5:11–14). When His Presence is acknowledged, those gathered are fundamentally there to receive any and all the aspects mentioned in Job 29. Jehovah is there (enthroned) to provide direction, comfort, rebuke, hope, grace, encouragement, prophetic insight, and purpose as only He can. He speaks, and we listen. Such impartations are given to those who are willing, ready, and able to receive whatever He gives. A phrase from a timeless hymn fits wonderfully here:

Strength for today, and bright hope for tomorrow
Blessings all mine and ten thousand beside.
~Thomas Chisholm, William Runyan
"Great is Thy Faithfulness" 1923

In summary, God doesn't *show up* when we beckon Him with our praises. He's already there! However, the manifestation(s) of His Presence are directly linked to our individual and corporate awareness of it. To the degree that we purpose to enthrone Him in/on our praises, He in turn inhabits what we build Him. From such a high and holy position, He then imparts what He chooses to, in any way He chooses, to whomever He chooses.

Let us become more aware of Your presence
Let us experience the glory of Your goodness.
~Bryan Torwalt, Katie Torwalt, "Holy Spirit"
Jesus Culture
(Admin. By Capitol CMG Publishing), 2011

What I'm addressing is this: The issue of God's abiding Presence isn't really an issue at all. Awareness of His Ever-Presentness is. (See Ps. 139:12; 1 Cor. 3:16.)

Selah (Pause & ponder.)

Enthroning God

I suppose we could imply that the third *why* we worship is based on the hope (expectation) that God will show up. But as I stated, He is everywhere, always present whether He manifests or not. The objective should be to learn how to listen and respond to what God says when He's enthroned among His people, rather than to concern ourselves with whether He'll manifest on any given Sunday morning.

However, many believers still speak of wanting God to "show up." You may have heard a pastor or a teacher state that the church needs a habitation from God, and not just a visitation. I'll add one more passage of Scripture to this mix to expand the context of what I'm saying. In 2 Chronicles 5:11–14, we're told this is what took place at the dedication of the Temple:

> *The priests then left the Holy Place. All the priests there were consecrated, regardless of rank or assignment; and all the Levites who were musicians were there—Asaph, Heman, Jeduthun, and their families, dressed in their worship robes; the choir and orchestra assembled on the east side of the Altar and were joined by 120 priests blowing trumpets. The choir and trumpets made one voice of praise and thanks to GOD—orchestra and choir in perfect harmony singing and playing praise to GOD. "Yes! GOD is good! His loyal love goes on forever!" Then a billowing cloud filled The Temple of GOD. The priests couldn't even carry out their duties because of the cloud—the glory of GOD!—that filled The Temple of God. (MSG)*

What we're looking at here is a worship service of monumental portion! Let's break it down:

All the priests are there, in place, and consecrated for whatever takes place next. The Levites are there as well, also ready for any service that the Spirit might begin to orchestrate. Musicians and singers abound—and their praise offerings are loud and filled with passion. Can you imagine what 120 trumpets would sound like in a Sunday service at your church?

The singers and musicians *"made one voice of praise and thanks to God."* In other words, they were not only prepared through consecration, but they were also unified in their sacrificial offerings. Then, the Holy Spirit began to change the atmosphere with the cloud of His Presence—the weightiness of His glory *(kabod* in Hebrew).

The very thing that the people had hoped would happen in fact did. But even though they had done their best to prepare for it, they still weren't ready for what took place. As a result, the service—for all practical purposes—was brought to an abrupt halt. The text says that no ministry was able to take place because the Lord took over. I wonder how many times comments are made in our churches about us being open and willing for the Lord to take over our services and do whatever He wants to do....

Here's the thing about that: The result of 2 Chronicles 5:14 was preceded by what took place in verses eleven through thirteen. Without the prep work transpiring first, why would we expect the same results to happen "in the house" when we gather for worship? If you've read your way to here, then you already know what the preliminary work was—consecration.

Now, let's get back to unpacking Psalm 22:3:

Part of the definition for *enthroning* (inhabiting) is that of a judge sitting in a position of authority. A better understanding of that might be to consider what a tribal chief does when he sits outside his hut. Those who live in the village gather before him to receive the counsel and direction he provides to the community at large. In other words, he takes his seat of authority to address the details of how the people are to conduct themselves with one another, live their lives, raise their families, and interact with other tribes within the region. Isn't that something we hope that the Lord will do for and with us?

> *"The steps of a good man are established by the Lord,"*
> ~Ps. 37:23a, NASB

> *"Establish my footsteps in Your word, and do not let any iniquity have dominion over me,"*
> ~Ps.119:133, NASB

Another aspect of this enthroning is to marry and set up housekeeping. The Hebrew language is very visual in its usage. The implication is that in doing so, the intention is to reside in one place—dwell—where an inviting and accommodating space has been set up, like, say, a throne. That dear reader, is what many of us say we want God to do: dwell among us. Not just come and visit, but rather, come and abide.

> Holy Spirit, You are welcome here
> Come flood this place and fill the atmosphere
> Your glory God, is what our hearts long for
> To be overwhelmed by Your presence, Lord
> ~Bryan Torwalt, Katie Torwalt, "Holy Spirit."
> Jesus Culture
> (Admin. by Capitol CMG Publishing), 2011

These lyrics speak directly to what God wants to do when He comes among us. Change the atmosphere, give direction to our lives (personally and corporately), and counsel us on how to maintain our communities. In essence, rule over and among us as our Sovereign! Do you see what I'm saying?

> Say what you hear, so that you can see what you say.
> ~Bishop Joseph Garlington

The next word in Psalm 22:3 to consider is the word *praises*. Note please, that it is not singular in its usage, it's plural. It is expressed regarding a group of people in song, not to an individual singing alone.

> *Where two are three have gathered in My name,*
> *I am there in their midst.*
> ~Matt. 18:20 NASB

In the Hebrew it is *tehillah*, meaning to laud or offer laudation.

It has to do with singing—but not singing singularly. It's not used here as personal, individual singing. It's referring to congregational singing. It takes place in corporate worship. Think of it as a "one voice" expression much like the dynamic expressed in the 2 Chronicles 5 passage I've already mentioned. It is not a passive word. Nor is it non-active—it's pro-active. It is filled with passion, zeal, and gusto. It comes from the base word *halah*, which means to shine; to make a show; to boast; to act clamorously foolish; to rave and celebrate; to act foolish (Strong's Bible Concordance). I'm not making this stuff up—*don't shout me down!*

> No chorus is too loud, no orchestra too large, no Psalm
> too lofty for the lauding of the Lord of Hosts.
> ~Charles Spurgeon

Between the word *enthroned* and the word *praises*, there is one more little word we need to consider. It's the word *on*. The verse says that God is enthroned *on* the praises of His people. What the word *on* tells us is that the throne itself is built out of (fashioned from) our praises. Yep, that's what it says.

You see, when we gather with the intentional purpose of enthroning God, we become throne builders. What we create with our sacrificial offerings of praise is somehow supernaturally transformed into the very seat of authority that God wants to come and occupy in the midst of us (Ps. 22:22–25; Ps. 116:19). Once seated there, all the things that He desires to impart to us as His people then begin to flow out of the Spirit directly into our lives (both personally and corporately). That is astounding. The possibilities are too breathtaking to imagine.

> On the whole, I do not find Christians, outside of
> the catacombs, sufficiently sensible of conditions. Does
> anyone have the foggiest idea what sort of power we so
> blithely invoke? Or, as I suspect, does no one believe

a word of it? The churches are children playing on the
floor with their chemistry sets, mixing up a batch of
TNT to kill a Sunday morning. It is madness to wear
ladies' straw hats and velvet hats to church; we should
all be wearing crash helmets. Ushers should issue life
preservers and signal flares; they should lash us to our
pews. For the sleeping god may wake someday and take
offense, or the waking god may draw us out to where
we can never return.

> ~Annie Dillard, "An Expedition to the Pole"
> *Teaching a Stone to Talk,* Harper & Row, 1982

Our finite ability to comprehend the eternal otherness of the
Trinity requires humility on our part before the Father, Son, and
Holy Ghost. It also calls for us to appropriate mercy and grace at
the throne of grace (*Heb. 4:16). Otherwise, to even try to reason
our way through to the unbounding expansiveness of the giver
and sustainer of life is presumptive religion.

*The word *need* in Hebrews 4:16 means well-timed opportunity.
It comes from a word meaning an occasion (Strong's Concordance).
I take that to mean that any time is the right time to implement
the directive in that verse. (See previous section in Part One, "The
Cycle of Hope.")

> *Now that we know what we have—Jesus, this great
> High Priest with ready access to God—let's not let it slip
> through our fingers. We don't have a priest who is out of
> touch with our reality. He's been through weakness and
> testing, experienced it all—all but the sin. So let's walk
> right up to Him and get what He is so ready to give. Take
> the mercy, accept the help.*
>
> ~Hebrews 4:14–16 MSG

The God of the Bible is relentlessly a political

character whose presence delegitimates wrong power arrangements, whose purposes summon and authorize new power arrangements... [T]he rhetoric of praise is an act of guerrilla warfare...it celebrates, acknowledges, and claims gifts and purposes that the world judges to be impossible. In its utterance of impossibility, it mocks and dismisses the conventional notions of possibility in which we trust too much... [T]hus praise, in asserting that new reality emerges around the character of God.

~Walter Brueggemann, *Our Hearts Wait*
Westminster John Knox Press, 2022

We see Jesus, His disciples, and multitudes of people in a similar dynamic scene as presented in Job 29. Considering Job 29 and Matthew 5:1–2 together can serve to focus and reinforce what's stated in Psalm 22:3.

Note to reader: The following Scriptural passage isn't presented here in its proper Biblical context. I'm including it regarding the concept of so-called *Worship Warfare*. Although that's not the topic of this manuscript, it nonetheless addresses a subject that merits further consideration. (See *Silencing the Enemy* by Robert Gay, Prophetic Praise Ministries, 1993.)

The Lord will get furious. His fearsome voice will be heard, his arm will be seen ready to strike, and his anger will be like a destructive fire, followed by thunderstorms and hailstones. When the Assyrians hear the Lord's voice and see him striking with his iron rod, they will be terrified. He will attack them in battle, and each time he strikes them, it will be to the music of tambourines and harps.

~Isaiah 30:30–32 CEV

Every Act of Worship
      (Isa. 30:31–32; 1 Sam. 14:1–14)

Every act of worship
Is an act of war
And every song of Zion
Is a weapon in that war
So join me on the battle line
And lift your voices up with mine
Every act of worship
Is an act of war

Every revelation
Every kingdom truth
Is a declaration
Of the Spirit's proof
So join me on the battle line
And lift your voices up with mine
Every act of worship
Is an act of war

Go up to the battle
Go up to the battle
Go up to the battle with me
DON'T BACK DOWN!
      ~W. Berry, See & Say Songs, BMI, 2007

Let's work on all this a little more...

If our praises are the substance from which the throne of praise is built, it would then follow that the amount of praise we bring with us "in the house" determines the size of the throne itself. Once construction is completed, the purpose of building it can then take place—which is to enthrone God. When He comes to sit on the throne we've built for Him, He will occupy it (or fill it) with His Divine Presence. Now, hold that thought as I share with you a story (a revelation) which applies specifically to what I'm sharing.

Years ago, I was reading a book by Tommy Tenney entitled, *God's Favorite House*. In it, there is a chapter called "Building A Mercy Seat." Although the focus of that chapter isn't about throne building as such, the story draws a parallel that has stuck with me till today:

Tenney once new a very large man at his church. In fact, the man was extremely overweight. During the time he was in fellowship there, he grew less and less sociable in terms of his interaction with others at the church. One day, Tenney took him aside and asked him why he had withdrawn from the relationships he'd been active in. The gentleman said that he'd had to stop going to people's homes when he was invited because when he got there, he couldn't find any place to sit down. There were simply no pieces of furniture large enough, or solid enough, to hold his weight. That made him sad, and it made those he had gone to visit uncomfortable—creating an awkward situation for everybody there. As a result, he just stopped going when he was invited.

That story applies to what I've been sharing in this manner: God's Presence, His glory *(kabod*—see 2 Chron. 5:14) is expansive and weighty. When He wants to manifest, His intention is to fill up the places where He is. So, the more room there is for Him to "show up," the more of Him will [in fact] show up.

Praise, our congregational praises, provide us with the materials to build a throne for our Sovereign to sit on as He dwells among us, imparting all the things we need to live as citizens of heaven, ministers of reconciliation, and ambassadors for Christ (see 2 Cor. 5:18–21).

"You realize, don't you, that you are the temple of God, and God Himself is present in you?"
~1 Cor. 3:16 The Message Bible

The Best Seat in the House
~Ps. 22:3

VERSE 1:
Make room, make way
We've come into this house to bless Him today
Make some noise, lift up a shout
Do what you've got to do to get your praises out

CHORUS:
(Our God deserves)
The best seat in the house
Lord come and take Your rightful place
You are due the highest honor
So we're building You a throne of praise
The heavens cannot contain You
Of that there is no doubt
We welcome Your holy Presence
(You deserve) The best seat in the house

VERSE 2:
Take a stand, make a choice
Open up the heavens with the sound of your voice
State it clear, say it plain
Do what you've got to do to declare Him as King
~W. Berry, See & Say Songs, BMI

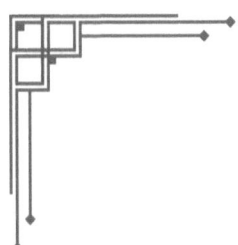

Part Four

WORSHIPPERS WILL WORSHIP

But the hour is coming, and is now here, when the true worshippers will worship the Father in spirit and truth, for the Father is seeking such people to worship him. God is spirit, and those who worship him must worship in spirit and truth.

~John 4:23–24

In the previous chapters, I've addressed three of the *whys* of worship. The progression began with the commandment to worship God (Deut. 5:7), to the necessity of the breath of life being essential in offering worship (Ps.150:6), and then on to corporate/congregational expressions of worship (Ps. 22:3). I'd like to look next at *why* worshippers do what they do, as well as *who* they are.

The Real Deal

Romans 12:1–2 defines how God-worshippers are to offer themselves to God—as a "living sacrifice." I'll address that in more detail in Part Five.

John 4:23–24 says that God Himself is seeking after a specific type of worshipper, those *"who will worship Him,"* not lesser (or false) gods (see Deut. 5:7). That implies that *all* people are worshippers—some who worship Him, and all the others who don't.

In verse twenty-three, the phrase *"worshippers who worship"* is easily overlooked. In it, *worshippers* are nouns (people), and *worship* is a verb (an action or actions). Worship (in various ways and means) is what worshippers manifest. The external expression(s) of worship are based on an internal reality.

"Right thinking of God, through the study and application of the word of God, renews our mind and informs our soul how to respond in worship."

~Jonathan Grisham, YouTube,
Springhouse Church Channel
"Worship," April 27, 2025

Now, we come to the concept of authentic worship as being the *real deal.* The best way I know to explain that is to consider these verses in John. Looking at each phrase separately may help to convey the concept I'm presenting.

"But the hour is coming and is now here…"

~Jn. 4:23

To establish the proper context for the content of that statement, it's necessary to turn our attention to the verses before it (Jn. 4:7–10). The interchange between Jesus and the woman at the well provides that context and requires some unpacking. The key aspects of their interchange are as follows:

1. Jesus makes a request for a drink from the woman who is drawing water from the well.
2. She begins an interchange regarding tribal differences and cultural dynamics.
3. Jesus responds to her comments by telling her that she's missing the point of their encounter entirely. He states that the *"gift of God"* that's being offered to her is a *Who*, and that He is [in fact] the *Who Himself*.

Read John 4:11–19 for the ongoing details of their conversation.

Thereafter, the story continues...

"Our fathers worshipped on this mountain, but you say that in Jerusalem is the place where people ought to worship." Jesus said to her, "Woman, believe me, the hour is coming when neither on this mountain nor in Jerusalem will you worship the Father. You worship what you do not know; we worship what we know, for salvation is from the Jews."

~John 4:20–22

The main thrust of the opening phrase, *"But the hour is coming, and now is..."* unfolds (finds fulfillment) in the comments Jesus makes in verse twenty-one. The woman is concerned with the *who*, *what*, and *where* of worship. However, Jesus is trying to focus her on the *why*. The revelation He is about to impart goes straight to the heart of the reason for act(s) of worship.

"...when the true worshippers will worship the Father in spirit and truth..."

v. 23b

73

The phrase, *"true worshippers will worship the Father,"* deserves much more attention than it is given in the preaching and teaching currently taking place in our corporate services, study groups, and private readings of Scripture. Over the past half century, I've noticed that most often what's addressed in that text is the *"spirit and truth"* aspect. However, that comes at the expense of overlooking the portion that says, *"true worshippers will worship."*

If the text says there are true worshippers, then false worshippers are implied. You can't have one without the other.

Here I'm referring to the theme of Chapter One. If you recall, I began with Deuteronomy 5:7 as the first *why* of worship. I view that as the place where the separation between true worship and false worship is first delineated. Now, look (again) at what both the Old and New Testaments say regarding worship of lesser gods (see Ps. 115:2–7 and Rom. 6:16).

The phrase being considered here, *"true worshippers will worship,"* is stating what should be (but isn't) an obvious fact:

Worship is what worshippers do. True God-worshippers offer up authentic worship to the "One True God." False worshippers offer up inauthentic worship to lesser (false) gods. That is idolatry in and of itself.

Spirit and Truth

Anything and everything that exalts itself against the knowledge of God is the exact opposite of how *"spirit and truth"* worship is to be offered.

Spirit: A current of air (breath), or a breeze; the rational soul; vital principle, mental disposition (i.e. the Holy Ghost)

Truth: Verity. From a word meaning something not concealed .(Strong's Bible Concordance)

> *"Casting down imaginations, and every high thing that exalts itself against the knowledge of God and bringing*

into captivity every thought to the obedience of Christ..."
~2 Cor. 10:5

Acts 1:8 conveys the same dynamic with the phrase, *"you shall be my witnesses...."* It states that the disciples will become witnesses—they will *be* witnesses. Witnessing is what witnesses do, not who they are. In the same way, *"worshippers will worship,"* because that's what worshippers do.

Selah (Pause & ponder.)

In 2 Corinthians 10:5, the phrase *"bringing into captivity every thought"* is related to a portion of the directive in Romans 12:1–2. Verse two says to *"be transformed by the renewing of your mind..."*

In Greek, the word *renewing* means renovation. Renovation is a process. It takes time, more time than confession does. Renovation takes however long it takes until the desired change has been accomplished. It has a beginning, a middle, and an end. Depending on the nature of the renovation, it could take weeks, months, years, or even longer.

In essence, the renewing of our minds is the root of the repentance process, from conviction to completion. Here's what that process looks like in Psalm 51, David's narrative of repentance: *Conviction to Confession to Repentance to Restoration to Renewal to Revival.*

"But the hour is coming, and is now here, when the true **worshippers will worship** *the Father in spirit and truth, for the Father is seeking such people to worship him,"*
~Jn. 4:23, emphasis added

Offering worship doesn't make someone a worshipper. Being a worshipper is what generates their acts (services) of worship. *"Worshippers will worship..."* That's what they do.

Worship is obedient service manifesting through self-sacrifice.

(Wayne-Speak; see Rom.12:1, MSG. Note: This verse contains the meaning of the word *worship*.)

Worship: To kiss (like a dog licking their master's hand); to fawn or crouch down to; to prostrate oneself in homage. From a word meaning to move forward, toward, or beside; near to in place, time, or occasion, which is the destination of the relationship. (Strong's Bible Concordance)

It is the same word (and definition) used every place in the book of Revelation. This means such action (with such meaning) is taking place in eternity (outside of and beyond temporal earth time), around the throne of God at the very moment you're reading this.

Note also that there is no mention of music or any other aspect of what we commonly consider to be worship. That's because the external components of worship—the manifestations—are (in a sense) fruits from the root. And the root isn't outward, it's inward.

Note to reader: A worthwhile source book regarding the aspects of worship is *Worship God: Exploring the Dynamics of Psalmic Worship* by Ernest B. Gentile, Bible Temple Publishing, 1994.

Who's Seeking Who?

Much of the narrative content offered through our contemporary preaching, teaching, and discussion groups—including the lyrics of many of our current *psalms, hymns, and spiritual songs*—speaks of the need to draw nearer to God by seeking His Presence. Those interchanges are (by and large) sincere in terms of intent. However, such rhetoric tends to create or sustain an imbalanced theology related to our personal and corporate worship. There are many verses and Scriptural passages that support such a perspective of seeking after God, or Jesus, or the Holy Ghost. For that reason, such an approach is certainly an acceptable approach to developing and sustaining a spiritually religious relationship. But there are a number of Biblically based statements that serve to point out the potential for misunderstanding the dynamics of what's presented in John 4:23–24.

Here's what I mean:

The words that follow the phrase, "*worshippers will worship*" read, "*God is seeking.*" Those words come directly from the mouth of Jesus as He explains a major aspect of worship—the *why* of it. In that narrative, He is saying that the reason spirit-and-truth worshippers should worship is so that God can/will find what He's seeking for. Or said another way, *who* He's looking for. *That is huge!*

Based on the language of that text, the seeking that is taking place is not what God-worshippers are doing. Rather, God Himself is the one on the lookout for specific types of worshippers. That POV reveals a much wider vista of what transpires when worshippers (in fact) worship. Even though the *who, what, when,* and *where* of worship are important considerations, the main aspect to ponder is *why* such sacrificial offerings should be happening.

Let's unpack this process further from a Scriptural viewpoint:

In John 4:7–20, the woman at the well is basing a portion of her interchange on *what, when,* and *where* of worship.

By doing so, she is positioning herself with God in terms of proximity. She wants to make the acquisition of facts and hard data *about* worship the main point of her involvement as a worshipper. In response, Jesus explains that an intimate relationship directly joined to Him is at the center of *why* worship should take place. He tells her directly that *if* she'll begin to worship the Father in the way that Jesus is encouraging, then God will seek her out. *Why?* Because that's the kind of worship that He is seeking from "*worshippers [who] will worship.*"

Are you trackin' with me here? I hope so.

Here are several verses to support what I've just presented:

"*I and the Father are one,*" (Jn. 10:30).

"*If you've seen me, you've seen the Father,*" (Jn. 14:9).

"*I will never leave you or forsake you,*" (Heb. 13:5).

Each of these verses speak directly about the unity between

the Father and Son. They make a case for the fact that the very person the woman is seeking is standing directly before her. To say that even more directly, she is speaking to Jehovah, but she doesn't know that she is. Jesus is drawing her into a heart-to-heart union that she has never experienced. She is on the verge of a supernatural breakthrough with "Otherness," based on the Divine encounter that's taking place. *Astounding!*

Let's continue.

In another place in Scripture, Jesus declares that He is *"the way, the truth, and the life,"* and that *"no one comes to the Father except through Me,"* (Jn. 14:6). Although this text places the responsibility of coming to God on those who will seek Him, it is based on the redemptive stage of salvation—accepting Christ as Savior. That step is the very first act of worship *after* a person is *"accepted in the Beloved,"* (Eph. 1:6). Thereafter, the seeking shifts from those who have (or will) receive Him, to God seeking for specific converts who have (or will) become spirit-and-truth worshippers. *Again, overwhelming!*

At Pentecost, the gift of the indwelling Presence, power, and purpose of the Holy Ghost was/is imparted to those who accept Him (Acts 1:8). Seeking some sort of manifested presence would at that point become redundant. There is no point in seeking something (or somebody) that's already present. When Presence is present, what's essential is to acknowledge that, and respond accordingly.

> *Do you not know that you are God's temple and that God's Spirit dwells in you?*
>
> ~1 Corinthians 3:16

> *If then you have been raised with Christ, seek the things that are above, where Christ is, seated at the right hand of God. Set your minds on things that are above, not on things that are on earth. For you have died, and your life is hidden*

with Christ in God. When Christ who is your life appears, then you also will appear with him in glory.

~Colossians 3:1–4

This Biblical data clearly expresses that God in Christ makes it possible for the Spirit to abide in us, and for us to be *"hidden with Christ in God."*

How much more present can Presence be?

"For in him we live and move and have our being,"

~Acts 17:28a

Notice how this process is rooted in the Old Testament as well:

Where shall I go from your Spirit? Or where shall I flee from your presence? If I ascend to heaven, you are there! If I make my bed in Sheol, you are there! If I take the wings of the morning and dwell in the uttermost parts of the sea even there your hand shall lead me, and your right hand shall hold me. If I say, "Surely the darkness shall cover me, and the light about me be night," even the darkness is not dark to you; the night is bright as the day, for darkness is as light with you.

~Psalm 139:7–12

He who dwells in the shelter of the Most High shall abide under the shadow of the Almighty.

~Psalm 91:1

Whom have I in heaven but you? And there is nothing on earth that I desire besides you. My flesh and my heart may fail, but God is the strength of my heart and my portion forever. For behold, those who are far from you shall

*perish; you put an end to everyone who is unfaithful to you.
But for me it is good to be near God; I have made the Lord
God my refuge, that I may tell of all your works.*
~Psalm 73:25–28

Remember that Jesus charged *all* who follow Him with a singular directive as the #1 Priority: Matthew 6:33 clearly states that our seeking is to be directed toward God's Kingdom and His righteousness.

Once we have sought out (and accepted) Christ Jesus as our Lord, and Savior, the seeking thereafter is on living in and out of the Kingdom. *If* in the process and practice of doing so, we become worshippers who will worship, the Trinity will do Their part to abide, dwell, lead, guide, and direct our path(s).

*Blessed are those whose strength is in you, in whose heart
are the highway(s) to Zion. As they go through the Valley
of Baca they make it a place of spring(s); the early rain also
covers it with pools. They go from strength to strength; each
one appears before God in Zion.*
~Psalm 84:5–7

(Note: Notice the plurals, they are important and far too often overlooked.)

Set Your Sights Above
~Col. 3:1–13

Set your *affections on things above
And not on earthly things
For you are dead and your life is hidden with Christ in God
So brothers be thankful and let His Word
Dwell in your hearts with love
Love one another, take care of each other
And set your sights above

If you are hidden in Christ your Savior
Then He is your all in all
And the peace of God dwelling in your hearts
Is the peace to which you're called
So sisters be thankful and let His Word
Work in your hearts with love
Love one another, take care of each other
And set your sights above

Learn charity through perfectness
Doing all in Jesus' name
Giving thanks to God in faithfulness
Bringing honor to His name
~W. Berry, See & Say Songs, circa 1983

*In the KJV, affections means to exercise the mind; to entertain or have sentiment or opinion toward; to be (mentally) disposed (more or less earnestly in a certain direction; to interest oneself in (with concern or obedience.

> "...[W]orshippers will worship..."
>
> ~Jn. 4:23

In the phrase above, *worshippers* is a noun. It is plural, meaning multiple people are said to be worshipping. It is a pro-active noun.

Worship herewith is a verb. The action(s) of worship (the expressions) are to be offered by those who *are*, in and of themselves, worshippers (see Rom. 12:1, MSG). In other words, worshippers carry worship inside (see Ps. 35:10a; 1 Cor. 3:16). Worship flows out of the lives of worshippers in the same fashion that witnessing flows out of a witness.

> "...and you shall be My witnesses..."
>
> ~Acts 1:8

There is a distinction between the word *witness* and the word *witnessing. Witness* is a noun. In the text above it is plural *(witnesses)*, meaning several people are designated to give testimony. It is to be considered as a pro-active noun.

The implication would be that *witnessing* is a verb. It is what a witness does. Witnessing flows out of a witness. Said another way, witnessing is proclaimed by a declaration from a witness. Worshippers worship. Witnesses witness.

Kingdom Coordinates (Proximity and Intimacy)

> When Jesus saw his ministry drawing huge crowds, he climbed a hillside. Those who were apprenticed to him, the committed, climbed with him. Arriving at a quiet place, he

sat down and taught his climbing companions.
> ~Matthew 5:1 MSG

What comes next is (Scripturally speaking) the Beatitudes and the Sermon on the Mount. The crowds were in geographic proximity to Jesus. The apprentices (student-disciples) were in relational intimacy with Him. There is a difference:

Proximity has to do with location (distance & accessibility).

Intimacy has to do with time spent in personal interaction.

Proximity takes place by being close by. Intimacy takes place by being close in.

Worship is obedient service manifesting through self-sacrifice.

> *So here's what I want you to do, God helping you: Take your everyday, ordinary life—your sleeping, eating, going-to-work, and walking-around life—and place it before God as an offering.*
> > Romans 12:1 MSG

> *And whatever you do, in word or deed, do everything in the name of the Lord Jesus, giving thanks to God the Father through him.*
> > ~Colossians 3:17

Both verses are rooted in the principle and practice of consecration. I define *consecration* as the setting apart of any person, place, or thing for acts of holy service. Here's how that is outworked:

In the King James Version, the Romans text states that we are to set ourselves apart as a *"living sacrifice."* That directs the focus to the personal aspect of consecration—the setting apart of any person. In Colossians 3:17, the text is focused on what a person does *"in word or deed."* Both of those aspects are things. A person's being (their body) occupies a place (or places), and their words and deeds are active wherever that may be. Therefore, our personage, and the actions of speaking and doing become expressed manifestations of consecration, as is stated in the context of these two verses. As a result of setting apart a person, along with their words and deeds, such consecration becomes holy service(s) of worship.

Such expressions of worship are external manifestations of an internal reality. Stated another way, a worshipper is someone who releases acts of worship through (or out of) who they are. What they say and do flows out from who they are.

DISCLAIMER(S)

1. Unpack what follows slowly. It contains more than meets the eye.
2. Every word of Scripture below is written to those who are *"hidden with Christ in God"* (Col. 3:3). It was/is not intended for the unredeemed.

Context: Everything that follows deals with process. None of it is based on salvation—which is a one-time event. Rather, it addresses an ongoing, *deliberate* response-ability of those to whom Paul is directing his remarks.

Romans 12:1 unpacks as follows:

> *"...[P]resent your bodies a living sacrifice, holy, acceptable unto God, which is your reasonable service,"*
>
> ~KJV

The English Standard Version translates *"reasonable service"* as *"spiritual service of worship."* That is the task the text is calling us to do. It is our action of daily surrender (consecration). Such action as that is how we become a *"living sacrifice."*

In other words, presenting ourselves makes us available to the Holy Ghost to do what He does—sanctification. Remember that sanctification takes place *after* salvation has occurred. As followers of Christ, we can choose not to yield to the Spirit's work of conforming us into the image of God's dear Son (Rom. 8:29). That will not affect our status as believers. However, it will affect how we live out our salvation while we are here on earth. *If* we submit ourselves to the workings of the Holy Ghost, He in turn can/will do the work of transforming us by the renewal of our mind.

RENEW MY MIND
~Rom.12:1, 2

Sometimes I'm feelin' down so low
I just can't face the day
The tempter's turned my heart so cold
And heaven seems so far away

But then I see where I've gone wrong
I've strayed away from you too long
I long to be where I belong
So down on my knees I pray
Lord Jesus, help me find my way

CHORUS:
Father renew my mind
Set my thoughts in the heavenlies
Father I've been so blind
Now I need the touch of your hand on me
Father open up my eyes
Help me see what you are doing
I'm willing just to be a part
Of how your Holy Spirit is moving
Father renew my mind, Father renew my mind
Heavenly Father, renew my mind

As a child of God I'm called to live
A life of love and grace
To give all that I have to give
Until I behold his face

But sometimes sin gets a hold on me
It won't let go and I can't get free

But my sweet Jesus rescues me
And every demon has to run
At the power in the name of God's Son

REPEAT CHORUS:
~W. Berry / See & Say Songs, BMI / Circa 1985

Now, consider Colossians 3:1–4 in *The Message:*

So, if you're serious about living this new resurrection life with Christ, act like it. Pursue the things over which Christ presides. Don't shuffle along, eyes to the ground, absorbed with the things right in front of you. Look up and be alert to what is going on around Christ—that's where the action is. See things from his perspective. Your old life is dead. Your new life, which is your real life—even though invisible to spectators—is with Christ in God. He is your life. When Christ (your real life, remember) shows up again on this earth, you'll show up, too—the real you, the glorious you. Meanwhile, be content with obscurity, like Christ.

Near the beginning of the passage is the conditional word *if.* (Remember it is addressing followers of Christ.) It is saying there is an option regarding those four verses. However, it is not stating that there is some sort of issue (or penalty) for not doing what the text says.

The intention of the passage is to help *renew (renovate) our minds* (which links directly back to Romans 12:2). This implies that we can live for Christ as His followers without ever having our minds renewed. There is an aspect of proximity and intimacy at work in a relationship such as that as well.

What follows is a brief series of postulations on the dynamics of worship:

Part #1

"By faith Jacob, when dying, blessed each of the sons of Joseph, bowing in worship over the head of his staff,"
~Heb.11:21

Chapter Eleven of the book of Hebrews is commonly referred

to as the "Faith Hall of Fame." Its narrative gives us many examples of those who lived their lives in and through faith. Some are known and named, others are only identified by their actions, remaining nameless (see verses 35–40).

Out of all the passages that address the subject of worship in the Torah (Old Testament scrolls), the author of Hebrews chose one singular story to comment on regarding that subject. It has it origin in Genesis 47:31 which states in part, *"[T]hen Israel bowed himself upon the head of his bed."*

The Hebrew wording for "bowed himself" basically means to prostrate oneself, before a monarch or superior in homage, as an act of worship. (Thayer's Greek English Lexicon) It corresponds to the word *worship* used in Genesis 22:5 which says, *"Then Abraham said to his young men, 'Stay here with the donkey; I and the boy will go over there and worship and come again to you.'"*

Based on the hermeneutical Principle of First Mention, its meaning can be understood as the fundamental way of relating to worship when used thereafter throughout Scripture. The internal root of worship is contained/explained in that definition. All the other external expressions of worship obtain their meaning(s) from the root meaning.

For a broader and more expansive vista: moving from temporal earthbound time all the way into boundless (open ended) eternity, consider Revelation 7:11, which states, *"[A]nd they fell on their faces before the throne and worshipped God...."* Note that the word *worshipped* conveys the same basic definition as Genesis 22:5, Genesis 47:31, and Hebrews 11:21.

Part #2

> *But an hour is coming, and is now here, when the true worshippers will worship the Father in spirit and truth. Yes, the Father wants such people to worship Him. God is spirit, and those who worship Him must worship in spirit and truth.*
> ~John 4:23–24 HCSB

This passage is a popular one in today's contemporary church gatherings. It's used a lot. However, it's stated more than studied. (At least it seems that way to me.) So, I'm going to unpack it a little. Looking at the content, we see the following aspects:

The worshippers mentioned are not the ones doing the seeking. Rather, God is the one in pursuit. He is looking for what might be called worship offered by authentic worshippers. Those who worship in *"spirit and truth."*

That being the case, it would be a good idea to know what *"spirit and truth"* mean, and not just quote the phrase and leave it at that. (This is exactly where I began this series of ponderings.)

If such authentic God-directed worship is resident inside a follower of Christ, then no external attributes are required or necessary. Scripture states clearly that God looks at the heart (1 Sam.16:7). However, there is another consideration for outward responses to manifest.

> *"[T]he mouth speaks what the heart is full of,"*
> ~Luke 6:45, NIV

That is to say, the external dynamics of worship most certainly have their place as expressions of what's taking place internally, inside the hearts of those who are by definition *"spirit and truth"* worshippers.

Part #3

In the Greek language of the New Testament (John 4), *"spirit and truth"* means the following:

Spirit: A current of air (breath), or a breeze; the rational soul; vital principle, mental disposition (i.e. the Holy Ghost)

Truth: Verity. From a word meaning something not concealed (Strong's Bible Concordance)

There is another component in the text that merits our attention. However, it's not written, it's implied. Based on the implications, it could read this way: From among *all* worshippers,

God is seeking a specific kind—those who willingly worship *Him* in *"spirit and truth."*

The text seems to be saying that everybody who has ever been born, who is living now, and will live in the future are [in fact] worshippers of something or somebody. Here's why I say that:

> *"You shall have no other gods *before Me,"*
>
> ~*Deut. 5:7*

*The NASB uses the word *besides* instead of *before*. I think that's a much better translation.

This verse deals directly with idolatry. Notice the distinction of God (capital *G*). That's Jehovah, the One True God. That's the same God who is said to be *"seeking"* in John 4:23. The verse draws on that distinction with the word *gods*—little *g* and plural—meaning multiple "lesser gods" (see Ps. 115:5–8 and Rom. 6:16).

With that in mind, the focus of John 4:23–24 becomes (or should become) clearer.

Part #4

Up to this point, the type of worship I've been addressing is internal. That's where the root of *"spirit and truth"* worship is found—inside of God-worshippers. Worship of that sort may (or may not) display any outward signs. Why? Because internal worship is not based on external evidence. It's based on internal residence, abiding and indwelling Presence (see Ps. 139:7–12 and 1 Cor. 3:16).

That brings me back to Revelation 7:11, which I mentioned in Part #1. You see, such worship—offered by such worshippers—not only takes place here on earth, but it also takes place off planet, in eternity, forever!

> *"...[T]rue worshippers will worship..."*

I call your attention to this simple fact: Worshippers worship.

That's what they do because that's who they are—worshippers. What they offer doesn't make them worshippers. They are [in fact] worshippers. Being worshippers is what gives them something to offer. Their internal lives enable them to offer external expressions of worship both now, and into their eternal future.

Worship is obedient service manifesting through self-sacrifice. (Wayne-Speak)

Just sayin'....

Embodiment In Action

> So here's what I want you to do, God helping you: Take your everyday, ordinary life—your sleeping, eating, going-to-work, and walking-around life—and place it before God as an offering. Embracing what God does for you is the best thing you can do for him. Don't become so well-adjusted to your culture that you fit into it without even thinking. Instead, fix your attention on God. You'll be changed from the inside out. Readily recognize what he wants from you, and quickly respond to it. Unlike the culture around you, always dragging you down to its level of immaturity, God brings the best out of you, develops well-formed maturity in you.
>
> ~Romans 12:1–2 MSG

Having focused much of my attention on the rendering of this passage in the Message Bible, I've addressed the Scriptural concepts of being a *"living sacrifice"*, as our *"reasonable service"* of *"spiritual worship."* Several other translations use that terminology.

My focus here is on two things specifically linked to that concept:

1. How Jesus embodies Romans 12:1
2. How ultimate freedom is directly linked to the worship that Jesus embodies

My definition of *worship* is obedient service manifesting through self-sacrifice.

That (in essence) is a distillation of what Romans 12:1 declares. Simply stated, Jesus did exactly what the text says worship is to be—a giving over of oneself in yielded/obedient service to God the Father.

A supporting text that speaks to that process is Philippians 2:5–8:

> *Have this mind among yourselves, which is yours in Christ Jesus, who, though he was in the form of God, did not count equality with God a thing to be grasped, but emptied himself, by taking the form of a servant, being born in the likeness of men. And being found in human form, he humbled himself by becoming obedient to the point of death, even death on a cross.*

When Jesus sacrificed His life (in obedient service), He was offering Himself in His earthly-living state of being. When He gave up His Spirit (*"it is finished,"* Jn. 19:30) and died, two things took place after He was buried:

1. He was resurrected into life after death (Rom. 8:29)
2. He came up from the netherworld with the keys to death and hell itself (Rev. 1:18)

He didn't just die, He killed death!

Those two aspects of worship opened the way for all who were to become followers of Christ to live in the freedom of life after death, in the same way that Jesus did. Our death and burial do not have to be exactly as His. However, the result will be the same: freedom from death, into the freedom of eternal life.

The death of God resulted in the death of death. The

death of God dooms death itself to its own undoing. The crucifixion of Christ was not a defeat that was overturned by resurrection. Rather it was a victory revealed in resurrection.

~Brian Zahnd, *The Wood Between the Worlds*
IVP, 2024

Christ is risen from the dead, trampling down death by death, and upon those in tombs bestowing life.

~Hilarion Alfeyev, *Christ the Conqueror of Hell: The Decent into Hades from an Orthodox Perspective.*
St. Vladimir's Seminary Press, 2009

Early Christian preachers were fond of speaking of the death of Christ as a kind of trick played on the devil. They spoke of the flesh of Christ as the bait on the hook of divinity. Because Jesus was mortal, he could be swallowed by death, but death could not digest divinity. The devil took the bait and swallowed the hook. Once divinity was swallowed by death, death itself became ill and doomed to die.

~B. Zahnd, *The Wood Between the Worlds*

"The Son of Man came not to be served but to serve and to give his life a ransom for many,"

~Mk. 10:45

Note to reader: For additional background consideration, see this link: https://www.christianity.com/wiki/jesus-christ/the-harrowing-of-hell-descent-of-christ-into-hades.html

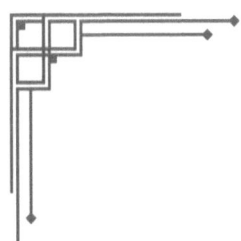

PART FIVE

OUR REASONABLE ACTS OF SERVICE

I beseech you therefore, brethren, by the mercies of God, that ye present your bodies a living sacrifice, holy, accept-able unto God, which is your reasonable service.
~Romans 12:1 KJV

In the previous chapters I've presented, four of the *whys* of worship have been my focus:

1. Worship is a command from God (the Creator of life) to counteract idolatry.
2. Everyone (everything) created carries the ability to offer worship, in varied ways and means. (See Ps.19:1-4; *Ps.104; Rom.1:20.)
3. The motivation to worship is extended to individuals as well as collective groups of people.
4. Worshippers will worship, because that's what they do.

*In his book, *Our Hearts Wait*, Walter Brueggemann has a wonderful exposition of Psalm 104. It's well worth reading.

This closing chapter addresses *why* those four dynamic services are to be offered as acts of worship. Because speaking Scripturally, doing so is our *reasonable service*.

Before I dive further into this chapter, I'll look deeper into a phrase in the verse that anchors it:

The phrase is *"living sacrifice."*

First, the language from Greek, according to Strong's Bible Concordance:

Living: From life; to live.

Sacrifice: From a word meaning to rush (to breathe hard); to blow smoke; to immolate (to slaughter by fire for any purpose).

When this phrase is considered in the context of the entire verse, we find that it is directly related to an act (or acts) of worship.

Here's where we go a little deeper...

As I've already stated, the first-time worship is mentioned Scripturally is in Genesis 22:5. Based on the principle and practice of first usage, it means that every manifested act of worship should be understood as being built upon the foundation of the original usage. In Hebrew, Strong's Bible Concordance identifies that definition as:

šāḥâ (pronounced *shaw-khaw'*): To depress; prostrate (in homage to royalty or God); to bow (self); crouch, fall down (flat); to humbly beseech; do reverence, make to stoop, worship.

If we look closely at the narrated scene in Genesis 22:5, we find that those gathered were all Hebrews, speaking the same language, and knowing the same cultural dynamics. With that in mind, we can extrapolate the following data points:

Abraham, Isaac, and the servants knew that worship involved (included) a sacrificial presentation.

Sacrificial worship required these components:

A. A sacrifice of some kind
B. Fire for burning the sacrifice up entirely
C. Wood for starting a fire
D. Some means of starting a fire
E. Some sort of tool for killing the sacrifice (if it was alive)

All those components were available when Abraham and Isaac started up the hill. The servants had no reason to discuss what was happening. They had taken part in such activities many times before. They had only to settle down and wait where they were until father and son returned from completing their offering. Therefore, the idea of a *"living sacrifice"* was clearly comprehended by everyone involved.

To continue...

In Psalm 141:2, David broke religious protocol by requesting of Jehovah, *"May my prayers be counted as incense before You; the lifting up of my hands as the evening sacrifice."* David wasn't a priest, so his request was technically out of order, a violation of procedure. Nonetheless, his plea was accepted based on what he voiced. Theologically speaking, I'm not prepared to say that what follows is Biblically correct. But I will nonetheless make this postulation:

David knew the story of Abraham and Isaac. He also knew that when the priests offered up their prayers in sacrifice, they were presented as incense lifted in bowls, while the sweet-smelling savor burned down into ashes. Such a scene as this could have been grounded in what took place at the first offering of worship mentioned Genesis.

From a New Testament perspective, Paul knew the Genesis story as well as David's request in Psalm 141. Both of those stories combined could have factored into his statement in Romans 12:1, linking his pronouncement to the Christians in Rome directly to Abraham's sacrifice, as well as to David's. (Although you may not agree with my sanctified imagination, there's a chance that it'll preach.)

And another angel came and stood at the altar with a golden censer, and he was given much incense to offer with the prayers of all the saints on the golden altar before the throne, and the smoke of the incense, with the prayers of the saints, rose before God from the hand of the angel.

~Revelation 8:3–4

One more observation before I move on…

Colossians 3:17 is one of the most important and impactive verses regarding the outworking(s) of worship:

> *"And whatever you do, in word or deed, do everything in the name of the Lord Jesus, giving thanks to God the Father through him."*

The concept of *all* aspects of *"word and deed"* being done in the name of the Lord as thanksgiving to God the Father, is as inclusive as possible concerning our attitudes and actions as worshippers (Ps. 136:1–3). What we say and do leaves little room for misunderstanding *where, how, what,* and *when* worship is to take place. All four of these aspects are contained and explained in the *whys.*

Eugene Peterson's rendering of Romans 12:1 provides a viewpoint of worship that links directly with the Colossians 3:17 text:

> *"So here's what I want you to do, God helping you: Take your everyday, ordinary life—your sleeping, eating, going-to-work, and walking-around life—and place it before God as an offering,"*
>
> ~MSG

Peterson's explanation of *offering* encompasses acts of *doing.* So do Abraham's and David's. Their *doings,* through their *"words and deeds,"* are manifestations of their lives as worshippers. Such worshippers are the kind that God Himself is seeking after. They are the kind said to be sacrificial in *"spirit and truth,"* (Jn. 4:23–24).

If I am offering my life in conjunction with the verses in Romans 12 and Colossians 3, I am doing so as a *"living sacrifice."* As such, I am moving in union with the events of Genesis 22 and Psalm 141. By grace, through hope, in faith, and trust, I am.

Serving, Singing, and Sojourning

The pathway of righteousness is a service road. Navigating it requires the traveler to learn how to discern the voice of the Holy Ghost and then to purpose to follow Him as directed—through obedience. The fundamental source of guidance and empowerment required along this "holy highway" is the impartation of grace.

*"But you will receive power **after** the Holy Spirit has come upon you, and you will be my witnesses in Jerusalem and in all Judea and Samaria, and to the end of the earth,"*
~Acts 1:8, emphasis added

Here's how I unpack this verse:

Presence precedes Power / Power prompts Witness / Witness proclaims Testimony / Testimony produces Revival / Revival helps fulfill God's will on earth as it is in heaven. (See Hebrews 2:10.)

For followers of Christ, the sojourn we're on takes us along that service road. It's an ancient path, a highway of holiness. It was established before the foundation of the earth, and it leads from where we are to where we have yet to be. Our guide and traveling partner is the Holy Ghost, and our destination is an eternal resting place.

"O Lord, I love the habitation of your house and the place where your glory dwells,"
~Psalm 26:8

"For the Lord has chosen Zion; he has desired it for his dwelling place: This is my resting place forever; here I will dwell, for I have desired it,"
~Psalm 132:13–14

"When the Spirit of truth comes, he will guide you into all the truth…"

~John 16:13a

"Stand at the crossroads and look; ask for the ancient paths, ask where the good way is, and walk in it, and you will find rest for your souls,"

~Jeremiah 6:16

The wilderness and the dry land shall be glad; the desert shall rejoice and blossom like the crocus; it shall blossom abundantly and rejoice with joy and singing. The glory of Lebanon shall be given to it, the majesty of Carmel and Sharon. They shall see the glory of the Lord, the majesty of our God. Strengthen the weak hands and firm the feeble knees. Say to those who have an anxious heart, "Be strong, fear not! Behold, your God will come with vengeance, with the recompense of God. He will come and save you." Then the eyes of the blind shall be opened, and the ears of the deaf unstopped; then shall the lame man leap like a deer, and the tongue of the mute sing for joy. For waters break forth in the wilderness, and streams in the desert; the burning sand shall become a pool, and the thirsty ground springs of water; in the haunt of jackals, where they lie down, the grass shall become reeds and rushes. And a highway shall be there, and it shall be called the Way of Holiness; the unclean shall not pass over it. It shall belong to those who walk on the way; even if they are fools, they shall not go astray. No lion shall be there, nor shall any ravenous beast come up on it; they shall not be found there, but the redeemed shall walk there. And the ransomed of the Lord shall return and come to Zion with singing; everlasting joy shall be upon their heads; they shall obtain gladness and joy, and sorrow and sighing shall flee away.

~Isaiah 35:1–10

And how blessed all those in whom you live, whose lives become roads you travel; They wind through lonesome valleys, come upon brooks, discover cool springs and pools brimming with rain! God-traveled, these roads curve up the mountain, and at the last turn—Zion! God in full view!

~Psalm 84:5–7 MSG

Each sojourning pilgrim has been given the appropriate preparation and traveling attire:

…[B]eauty for ashes, the oil of joy for mourning, the garment of praise for the spirit of heaviness; that they might be called trees of righteousness, the planting of the Lord, that he might be glorified.

~Isaiah 61:3

I will greatly rejoice in the Lord; my soul shall exult in my God, for he has clothed me with the garments of salvation; he has covered me with the *robe of righteousness, as a bridegroom decks himself like a priest with a beautiful headdress, and as a bride adorns herself with her jewels.

~Isaiah 61:10

*Consider the word *robe* in this context:

"Let us rejoice and exult and give him the glory, for the marriage of the Lamb has come, and his Bride has made herself ready; it was granted her to clothe herself with fine linen, bright and pure"—for the fine linen is the righteous deeds of the saints.

~Revelation 19:7–8

This same glory road can/does on occasion lead directly into

101

battlefields of spiritual warfare. When such confrontations take place, a change of clothes is also made available:

> *Put on the whole armor of God, that you may be able to stand against the schemes of the devil. For we do not wrestle against flesh and blood, but against the rulers, against the authorities, against the cosmic powers over this present darkness, against the spiritual forces of evil in the heavenly places. Therefore, take up the whole armor of God, that you may be able to withstand in the evil day, and having done all, to stand firm. Stand therefore, having fastened on the belt of truth, and having put on the breastplate of righteousness, and, as shoes for your feet, having put on the readiness given by the gospel of peace. In all circumstances take up the shield of faith, with which you can extinguish all the flaming darts of the evil one; and take the helmet of salvation, and the sword of the Spirit, which is the word of God, praying at all times in the Spirit, with all prayer and supplication. To that end, keep alert with all perseverance, making supplication for all the saints...*
>
> ~Ephesians 6:11–18

"Grace is the divine favor of God's empowering Presence, enabling me to be who He created me to be, so I can do what He calls me to do."

~J. Ryle

As I understand grace, it is received in three distinct ways:
1. As a salvific gift (Eph. 2:8)
2. Through solicitation and appropriation (Heb. 4:16)
3. So-called Common Grace—given by the Grace Giver to whomever He decides to impart it to, whenever, wherever, and however He chooses

Lead Me to the Light
~Ps.16:11; 27:11; 119:33–40

Lead me in the path of the righteous
For Your name's sake, for Your name's sake
Oh, lead me in the way everlasting
For the glory of Your kingdom
O Lord, my God

CHORUS:
'Cause I don't want to lose my way
And wind up in the wilderness
Hear this prayer I pray
Order my steps upright
No, I don't want to lose my way
And wind up in the wilderness
Guide my steps each day
Lead me to the light
~W. Berry, See & Say Songs, BMI

Complementary to this daily and sometimes laborious service is that experience of God, *hitlahavut*, the going out of self, the "taste and see how good God is," that engenders a joy that seems to belong to another realm. The peak moments of ecstasy will be few and brief, but the memory of them abides, and something deep within us says that all the strivings of life are worthwhile because of them. The joy of these moments continues to flow as a deep, abiding current in our lives, to be called forth through devotion and service.

Hitlahvut is a Hebrew word that literally means "being aflame" or "to be on fire with God." It can also be translated as enthusiasm, excitement, passion, or rapture. The word comes from the linguistic root *lahav*, which means flame.

~Pennington, M. Basil, *A Place Apart*
Doubleday, 1983

It is the feeling that arises from contact with the light or fire of a spiritual source, and once kindled, the Divine flame is said to captivate forever.

~AI Overview

Corridor of Light

~Isa. 2:2–5

If I'm in a bad circumstance, with very few choices
Caught up in the chaos, and hearing strange voices
There's a path that I can take; It's a way for me to go
Down the corridor of light, there's a hand that I can hold

CHORUS:
When I'm liftin' up Jesus
When I'm liftin' up Jesus
When I'm liftin' up Jesus
I'm takin' demons down

Even at the end of the age, there's a promise I can claim
I can dignify my trials, when I call upon His name
Then in the middle of the warfare, or at the end of my rope
I'll see the corridor of light, where there's a glimmer left of hope

Repeat CHORUS

(We're movin') from glory to glory, from strength to strength
From one level to another, we're all done with unbelief
With our eyes on Zion, God's holy hill
We'll see the corridor of light, that shines and always will

~W. Berry, See & Say Songs, BMI

There's a phrase in the Romans 12 passage that the Message Bible renders as follows:

> *"Embracing what God does for you is the best thing you can do for him."*

However, in making a connection to the *why* of worship, there are other translations that are somewhat clearer and deserving of our attention:

> *"... which is your reasonable service" (KJV)*
> *"... which is your spiritual service of worship" (NASB)*
> *"... which is your spiritual worship" (ESV)*
> *"... this is your true and proper worship" (NIV)*
> *"... which is your rational (logical, intelligent) act of worship" (Amplified Bible)*
> *"... which is your rational worship" (Jubilee Bible 2000)*

As Bob Dylan so aptly observed in his song, "Gotta Serve Somebody," we all serve someone—whether it is God or the devil is a choice we make.

A Son's Reward

~Rom. 5:12–23

Sin entered the world through one man
Death entered the world through sin
In this way all men died
Because all men have sinned
But the gift of God is eternal life
Through Jesus Christ our Lord
Those who yield to do God's will
Receive a son's reward

~W. Berry, See & Say Songs, BMI

The passage from Romans 12, along with the Dylan quote and my own lyrics, share a commonality with each of the verses that anchor the previous four chapters. All the data that's presented is written for (and to) a collective group of people.

It can/should be applied to individuals, but it is intended first and foremost to be processed by a community of believers. In this chapter, I'll be addressing some of the aspects that fit into that Biblical framework.

In Chapter 1, the word *Thou* in Deuteronomy 5:7 translates as *You*, but not *You* as an individual. Rather, *You* in a collective/group sense. "*You shall have no other gods before me,*" (NIV).

In Chapter 2, the word *everything* in Psalm 150:6 covers *all* living things. Individuals are included in that concept, but the text is (again) directed to a group or grouping. "*Let everything that has breath praise the Lord,*" (NKJV).

In Chapter 3, Psalm 22:3 speaks of building a throne out of the praises of Israel. That's another example of corporate/congregational interaction. "*Yet you are holy, enthroned on the praises of Israel,*" (ESV).

In Chapter 4, the John 4:23 text is spoken by Jesus directly to a singular woman, but it is referring to all true worshippers of the one true God. "*But the hour is coming, and is now here, when the true worshippers will worship the Father in spirit and truth, for the Father is seeking such people to worship him,*" (ESV).

Another Scriptural example of inclusiveness is found in Philippians 2:12b that says, "*work out your own salvation with fear and trembling.*" The entire chapter (and the entire book) are written to the congregation in Philippi. Its directive is to be appropriated and applied by the members within that group, but the text is for the entire collective.

The Bible is filled with verses and passages that are purposed to provide corporate directions (2 Timothy 3:16–17). Disregarding their proper context can change the way the content is understood. However, using them for individual apportion shouldn't change their original intent. When applying verses (and passages) of Scripture personally, doing so should not disregard the collective grouping that they were intended for.

Doing What's Expected (Response-ability)

There are numerous portions of Scripture that address the *what's, how's, where's,* and *when's* of Christ's work on earth. Thus far in my narratives I've mentioned some of them. However, the five *whys* continue to be the reason for my personal postulations. Here's my last one, and it's EXTRA LARGE!

> *"[B]ut he said to them, 'I must preach the good news of the kingdom of God to the other towns as well; for I was sent for this purpose,"*
>
> ~Lu. 4:43

In this verse, Jesus tells us directly one of the things He came to do: *"preach the good news of the kingdom of God."* But the next phrase takes us to the heart of the *why* by stating, *"for I was sent for this purpose."* That's where my focus is centered with what's to follow.

Clearly one of the things Jesus came to do is addressed directly. That's where we see what one of His *job descriptions was/is. The *why* is expressed in what He says was His purpose—He was sent.

*2 Corinthians 5:18–21 details two aspects of living as followers of Jesus. In essence it imparts a directive to *all* who intend to function in service for the Lord. The charge is two-fold:

1. The ministry of reconciliation (job description)
2. Ambassadorship for Christ (job title)

According to Thayer's Greek English Lexicon, the word for *sent* is *apostello*. It means set apart; to send out; (on a mission); to go forth or out. It comes from a combination of two words:

Apo, which means to go off or away from something near, in various senses (of place, time, or relation) ... and *stello,* meaning to set fast; to abstain from associating with; to withdraw the self. These combined definitions provide an enlargement of what it means to be sent.

The Greek word for an *apostle* is *apostolos*. It means a delegate; an ambassador of the Gospel (officially a commissioner of Christ) with miraculous powers; a messenger.

When all these expansive meanings are unified, we see that Jesus was sent as the first (or Chief) Apostle.

> *"Therefore, holy brethren, partakers of the heavenly calling, consider the Apostle and High Priest of our confession, Christ Jesus..."*
>
> ~Heb.3:1, NKJV

Functioning in the position of Chief Apostle, Jesus came to earth in obedience to His Father's will and direction. That means He came to serve God's will. In doing so we are shown *why* that took place. He came (as a servant) to serve.

Great High Priest
~Heb.4:14–16

There is a Great High Priest
In the most holy place
Who has been touched by our infirmity
His name is Jesus, He intercedes for us
Before the Father, seeking His grace

Oh the beauty of His holiness
Oh the splendor of His righteousness
Christ our Savior, Lord and Master
True Messiah, the Great High Priest

There is a Great High Priest
In the most holy place
He sacrificed His life to save humanity
His name is Jesus, He ever pleads for us
Before the Father, seeking His grace

Oh the grandeur of His majesty
Oh the wonder of His love for me
Christ of Savior, Lord and Master
True Messiah, the Great High Priest
~W. Berry / See & Say Songs, BMI / Circa 1999

Here's some additional support from Scripture:

"Let love be genuine. Abhor what is evil; hold fast to what is good. Love one another with brotherly affection. Outdo one another in showing honor. Do not be slothful in zeal, be fervent in spirit, serve the Lord."
~Rom. 12:9–11, emphasis added

"For even the Son of Man came not to be served but to serve, and to give his life as a ransom for many."
~Mark 10:45

"For you were called to freedom, brothers. Only do not use your freedom as an opportunity for the flesh, but through love serve one another."
~Gal.5:13

"Have this mind among yourselves, which is yours in Christ Jesus, who though he was in the form of God, did not count equality with God a thing to be grasped, but emptied himself, by taking the form of a servant, being born in the likeness of men. And being found in human form, he humbled himself by becoming obedient to the point of death, even death on a cross."
~Phil.2:5–8

"As each has received a gift, use it to serve one another, as good stewards of God's varied grace."
~1 Peter 4:10

Abba Father gave His Son (Christ Jesus) a task to fulfill. Jesus, in turn, passed that same response-ability to His disciples with an apostolic impartation stated in the pre-Pentecostal pronouncement of Acts 1:8. This apostolic role (the sending) took place *after* the Holy Ghost was (in turn) sent to indwell not only the original twelve disciples, but also those who became disciples through their ministry of apostolic service. By extension, that same charge continues to be imparted still today to all those who enter the kingdom of God through their relationship with Christ (as their Lord and Savior), and through the indwelling of the Spirit (1 Cor. 3:16).

When We Worship

When we worship, we are changed
When we come into God's Presence
We will never be the same
When we worship, we are changed

When we worship, we are changed
Transformed into His image
In His likeness to remain
When we worship, we are changed

So let us worship Him
Lift up our hands to Him
Come let us worship Him
Cast all our cares on Him

~W. Berry, See & Say Songs, BMI

To the Least of These

> *"For I was hungry and you gave me food, I was thirsty and you gave me drink, I was a stranger and you welcomed me, I was naked and you clothed me, I was sick and you visited me, I was in prison and you came to me." Then the righteous will answer him, saying, "Lord, when did we see you hungry and feed you, or thirsty and give you drink? And when did we see you a stranger and welcome you, or naked and clothe you? And when did we see you sick or in prison and visit you?" And the King will answer them, "Truly, I say to you, as you did it to one of the least of these my brothers, you did it to me."*
>
> ~Matthew 25:35–40

In this passage we see that those who had been serving the Lord didn't realize that they were doing so. It's a prime example of how the service of worship can take place when the motivation is based on drawing little (or no) attention to yourself.

> *"And whatever you do, in word or deed, do everything in the name of the Lord Jesus, giving thanks to God the Father through him,"*
>
> ~Col. 3:17

> *"He must increase, but I must decrease,"*
>
> ~Jn. 3:30

A very important explanation of how the process of learning to serve is outworked is presented in Ephesians 4:10–16:

> *He who descended is Himself also He who ascended far above all the heavens, so that He might fill all things. And He gave some as apostles, and some as prophets, and*

115

*some as evangelists, and some as pastors and teachers, for
the equipping of the saints for the work of service, to the
building up of the body of Christ; until we all attain to
the unity of the faith, and of the knowledge of the Son of
God, to a mature man, to the measure of the stature which
belongs to the fullness of Christ. As a result, we are no
longer to be children, tossed here and there by waves and
carried about by every wind of doctrine, by the trickery of
men, by craftiness in deceitful scheming; but speaking the
truth in love, we are to grow up in all aspects into Him
who is the head, even Christ, from whom the whole body,
being fitted and held together by what every joint supplies,
according to the proper working of each individual part,
causes the growth of the body for the building up of itself
in love.*

~NASB

These verses are sequential. When considered (and applied)
in order, they move from the beginning of the process (v.10) to
the end of it (v.16). The process does not (and will not) function
properly unless the steps are followed in order of appearance and
appropriation. If a verse (or verses) is skipped over or passed by,
the desired goal will not be reached.

Here's an overview of what that passage presents:

V.11—The giving out of ministry response-ability was done
by Jesus. The so-called *Five-Fold Ministries* were given to *some*,
not to everyone.

V.12—Those ministries were given *"for the equipping of the
saints for the* **work of service**, *to the building up of the body of Christ,"*
(emphasis added).

V.13—That is to be done *"until we all attain to the unity of the
faith, and of the knowledge of the Son of God, to a mature man, to the
measure of the stature which belongs to the fullness of Christ."*

V.14—The result of such instruction (teaching, discipleship) is that the body of believers will *"no longer be children, tossed here and there by waves and carried about by every wind of doctrine ..."*

The next verse shifts from what needs doing and how it's to be done, to the *why* of the process:

V.15—*"...but speaking the truth in love, we are to grow up in all aspects into Him who is the head, even Christ...according to the proper working of each individual part, causes the growth of the body for the building up of itself in love."*

In essence, the so-called Five-Fold Ministries were given to some for the equipping of the many. Such equipping instruction (by example) is to take place for the entire collective of people (both leadership and those being equipped) to grow into maturity together. The resulting outcome is that the whole (entire) body of Christ (the church) is filled and held together by what *every* member provides, through the proper working of *everyone*. That in turn will cause the fellowship of believers to grow *together* and be able to build itself up in love.

Notice two things in particular:

The entire process involves the entire fellowship (leaders and congregation together). The dynamic isn't structured as two groups (leaders and those being led). It is a collectively combined organization.

Work (or works) of service is the critical component in operation (v.12), to bring about the hoped-for results (vs.15–16).

For reasons too numerous to address here, I believe the Ephesians process has broken down in our so-called Contemporary Christian Congregations. Briefly, here's why I say that:

The so-called Five-Fold Ministry roles are both distinct and collective at the same time. Each ministry has specific anointings, giftings, and responsibilities. However, they are charged (together) with equipping the saints to serve as they help raise them up into maturity.

In the phrase *"work of service"* (*"work of the ministry"* in the KJV)—the language carries the following meanings:

Work: To toil (as an effort or occupation); to labor.

Ministry: To attend to as a servant; to give aid or relief. That comes from a root word meaning to run errands; attend to (as a waiter at a table or in other menial duties).

(From Strong's Bible Concordance)

These definitions—in and of themselves—say nothing about apostleship, prophecy, evangelism, pastoral positions, or teaching gifting or assignments. Although each of the categories is Biblically assigned, the application of each one shares in the same charge: They are to function to grow saints up and help them learn (by example) how to serve people.

I think we should consider taking another look at how the process was designed to operate and what its goal is.

Just sayin'...

Just to Worship You
                    ~Eph. 1:21

Far above the heavens, and over all the earth
You, O Lord, are worthy to be praised
Through the grace You've given
We come before Your throne
Seeking to behold Your face

CHORUS:
Abiding in the shadow of Your Spirit
Hiding in the shelter of Your name
We have come by faith into this holy place
Just to worship You, just to worship You
We are here just to worship You

Far above all rulers, authorities and powers
You, O Lord, it's You alone who reigns
Through the grace You've given
We bow before Your throne
Honoring Your holy name

Repeat CHORUS
                    ~W. Berry, See & Say Songs, BMI

No Servant Is Above Their Master

> *When he had washed their feet and put on his outer garments and resumed his place, he said to them, "Do you understand what I have done to you? You call me Teacher and Lord, and you are right, for so I am. If I then, your Lord and Teacher, have washed your feet, you also ought to wash one another's feet. For I have given you an example, that you also should do just as I have done to you. Truly, truly, I say to you, a **servant** is not greater than his master, nor is a messenger greater than the one who *sent him. If you know these things, blessed are you if you do them."*
>
> ~John 13:12–17 emphasis added

*Apostolos: A delegate; An ambassador of the Gospel; a messenger. (Thayer's Greek English Lexicon)

The servanthood role that Jesus accepted from the Father in Luke 4:43, is the same charge that He passed along to His disciples. He did so by backing up His verbal pronouncement with His physical actions. That is, after all, how servanthood is outworked—by example.

I'll close this work by revisiting how it began—pondering the principle and practice of consecration. To do so, I will link it with what I've presented in this chapter:

Consecration is the setting apart of any person, place or thing for acts of holy service. (Wayne-Speak)

To be clear, holy service is not only the focus here, but also the likely foundational bedrock that worship is built upon. All five *whys* of worship are established upon the foundation of which Christ is the Cornerstone.

> *This Jesus is the stone that was rejected by you, the builders, which has become the cornerstone. And there is salvation in*

no one else, for there is no other name under heaven given among men by which we must be saved.

~Acts 4:11–12

"Jesus didn't come to make the world different, He came to make a different world."

~E. Stanley Jones

Creator God, Abba Father, consecrated His Son (Christ Jesus) by setting Him apart for acts of holy service. Jesus (as Chief Apostle) obeyed the Father by coming (being sent) as a servant—a *"suffering servant,"* (Isa. 53). Then, He charged His disciples to serve Him by serving others. And by extension, *all* those who are *"hidden with Christ in God"* have the same directive at work in their lives as well. (See Col. 3:1–4 and 2 Cor. 5:18–21.)

Very Good God

I must decrease and He must increase
That's how it's meant to be
I will bow before Him now
Declaring Him holy

BRIDGE:
For He alone is worthy
Worthy to be praised, He alone is righteous
Blessed be His name

CHORUS:
What a very good God He is, what a very good God
What a very good God He is, what a very good God

I must decrease and He must increase
That's alright with me
I will yield to His will
And let Him have His way with me

Repeat BRIDGE and CHORUS
~W. Berry, See & Say Songs, BMI

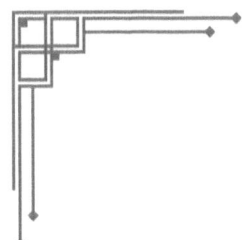

Addendum

The focus of what you've been reading is on five of the *whys* of worship. There are certainly more for consideration. I briefly addressed a few aspects of *how, what, when, where,* and *who as well.* That was intentional. My purpose isn't to sort out the external forms or factors of worship as they are commonly understood and expressed in churches today. Rather, I've unpacked five specific Biblical reasons for worship as topics of consideration.

I mentioned the concept of worship and praise being distinct, not separate. I also addressed the importance of content and context. Both narratives are subsets regarding the subject of worship. But, the musical expressions of styles, forms, musicianship, vocal approaches, tempos, volume levels, team leadership, membership participation, melodic composition, and such were purposely avoided. The so-called *"Worship Wars"* are not my concern.

There are already multiple books, podcasts, seminars, sermons, and teachings available that address those subjects.

However, while I have your attention, I'm providing some input about the intention(s) involved in conceiving and composing the songs we sing during our congregational *worship services.*

Here's the reason:

The *why* of writing *"psalms, hymns, and spiritual songs"* is (or should be) based on the intent of the person (or persons) composing the songs (see Eph. 5:19). Simply stated, the intent of the heart (through relational intimacy) is the starting point for such creative endeavors.

"...for out of the abundance of the heart his mouth speaks,"
~Luke 6:45c

Sojourner's Song Source

"Thy statues have been my songs in the house of my pilgrimage,"

~Ps. 119:54, DBY

In what follows, I am not suggesting that the reading of the Bible is to take place simply to acquire inspirational material for composing songs. That process should be a by-product of living in and out of Scripture because it contains the word(s) of life. It is daily manna, our bread of heaven. David says that it is, *"a lamp to my feet and a light to my path," (Ps. 119:105)*.

Thus says the Lord: This is what the LORD says: "Stand at the crossroads and look. Ask for the ancient paths: 'Where is the good way?' Then walk in it, and you will find rest for your souls...

~Jeremiah 6:16 BSB

And how blessed all those in whom you live, whose lives become roads you travel; They wind through lonesome valleys, come upon brooks, discover cool springs and pools brimming with rain! God-traveled, these roads curve up the mountain, and at the last turn—Zion! God in full view!

~Ps.84:5–7 MSG

NOTE: The destination is Zion (the principle). The routes are the road(s) (precepts). More on that just ahead.

Using God's word(s) as some sort of rhyming dictionary or considering it as an anointed thesaurus is an absurdly misguided approach for creating songs to sing "in the house."

*Your **testimonies** are wonderful; therefore, my soul keeps them. The unfolding of your **words** gives light; it imparts understanding to the simple. I open my mouth and pant, because I long for your **commandments**. Turn to me and be gracious to me, as is your way with those who love your name. Keep steady my steps according to your promise, and let no iniquity get dominion over me. Redeem me from man's oppression, that I may keep your **precepts**. Make your face shine upon your servant, and teach me your **statutes**. My eyes shed streams of tears, because people do not keep your **law**.*

~Psalm 119:129–136 emphasis added

Regarding Psalm 119, here is some insight from *The Treasury of David* by Charles Spurgeon (published between 1865–1885):

There is no title to this Psalm, neither is any author's name mentioned. It is *THE LONGEST PSALM*, and this is a sufficiently distinctive name for it. It equals in bulk twenty-two psalms of the average length of the Songs of Degrees.

Nor is it long only; for it equally excels in breadth of thought, depth of meaning, and height of fervor. It is like the celestial city which lieth four square, and the height and the breadth of it are equal. Many superficial readers have imagined that it harps upon one string and abounds in pious repetitions and redundancies, but this arises from the shallowness of the reader's own mind: those who have studied this divine hymn, and carefully noted each line of it, are amazed at the variety and profundity of the thought. Using only a few words, the writer has produced permutations and combinations of meaning which display his holy familiarity with his subject, and the sanctified ingenuity of his mind. He never repeats himself; for if the same sentiment recurs it is placed in a fresh connection and so exhibits another interesting shade of meaning. The more one studies it the fresher it becomes. As those who drink the Nile water like it better every time they take a draught, so does this Psalm become the fuller and fascinating the oftener you turn to it. It contains no idle word; the grapes of this cluster are almost bursting full with the new wine of the kingdom. The more you look into this mirror of a gracious heart the more you will see in it. Placid on the surface as the sea of glass before the eternal throne, it yet contains within its depths an ocean of fire, and those who devoutly gaze into it shall not only see the brightness but feel the glow of the sacred flame. It is loaded with holy sense and is as weighty as it is bulky. Again, and again have we cried while studying it, "Oh the depths!" Yet these depths are hidden beneath an apparent simplicity, as Augustine has well and wisely said, and this makes the exposition all the more difficult. Its obscurity is hidden beneath a veil of light, and hence only those who discover it who are in thorough earnest, not only to look on the word, but, like the angels, to look into it....

[T]he fashion among modern writers is, as far as possible, to take every Psalm away from David. As these critics are usually unsound in doctrine and unspiritual in tone, we suspect everything that comes from them. We believe David wrote this Psalm. It is Davidic in tone and expression, and it tallies with David's experiences. In my youth, our teachers called it "David's pocket book." We are of the opinion that this is a royal diary written at various themes throughout a long life. We cannot give up this Psalm to the enemy. "This is David's spoil." After reading an author, one gets to know his style, and a measure of discernment is acquired that detects his composition even if his name is concealed. We feel a critical certainly that David's hand is in this, and that it is altogether his.

I see Psalm 119 from the same perspective as Spurgeon. It is a love letter from David to Jehovah, expressing in considerable detail how much he loves God's Word(s). Today, and over far too many decades, followers of Christ have allowed the dumbing down of language to steal much of the depth and beauty of words, and to lose their impact in terms of meaning.

Personally, I believe that the dynamic of "dumbing down" is the work of the enemy of our souls. Words, and their misuse, is what was used in "The Garden" to set up "The Fall."

Now, in the era we live in when we express our love for the Scriptures, we tend to let one generic term serve as sufficient. We simply say "Word" and leave it at that. The use of *Word* has become a catch-all term.

David, however, utilized several words to express his affection for the Scriptures. And each one has its own meaning and application. In fact, he says that God's statutes had been the source of his songs throughout his pilgrimage. Here are the words he uses in Psalm 119 to express himself regarding his affection for the Word:

Laws: Torah; A precept, or statue.

Testimonies: Witnessing. From a word meaning to record or present.

Commandments: Laws, ordinances; precepts. From a word meaning to constitute, enjoin, appoint, bid, to send a messenger, to put in order.

Precepts: To appoint; a mandate from God.

Statutes: To appoint (of time, place, space, quantity, labor or usage); to decree as a task.

Judgments: A verdict (favorable or unfavorable); pronounced judicially (especially a sentence or formal decree); a divine law (individually or collectively); a particular right or privilege.

Word(s): A spoken matter; advice or counsel.
Ordinances: A determination; penalty; charge.
Principles: The first in place, time, order or rank. A firstfruit; beginning or chief thing.

~Strong's Bible Concordance

One of the most well respected and prolific commentators on Biblical worship is S.D. Gordon. The following quote is taken from his book entitled *Quiet Talks on The Crowned*, published in 1914. His works (in print) are astounding. Many of them are available in audio renderings as well, accessible on YouTube. A selection of his addresses can be found in a book entitled *The Collection*. I encourage you to get a copy.

On the mere human side here is one secret of the freshness of the Bible. It is the oldest book in some of its parts but admitted to be the freshest and most modern in its adaptation to modern life. And the reason is simple. The pictures give principles. Principles don't change with the changing of centuries. Rules change. Principles abide. Details alter with every generation. Principles of action are as unchangeable as human nature, which is ever the same, east and west, below the equator, and above.

With that in mind, here are my working definitions for *principle* and *precept:*
A **principle** is a goal (accomplishment/destination) that is intended to be reached. Think of it as the top of a mountain.
A **precept** is a way (or ways) of reaching that goal. Think of it as a pathway (or pathways) to reach the mountaintop.
David's primary motive for his creative compositions (his intent, his heart's desire) was, first and foremost, to offer the songs he wrote as vertical offerings to Jehovah (Ps. 141:2). There was

no thought given to copyright issues, publishing ownership, retail sales graphs, artistic recognition, or fame and fortune.

The secondary reason for his songs was likely to have them distributed horizontally to like-spirited worshippers for their own sacrificial offerings (Jn. 4:23–24).

I'm not saying that modern-day music industry concerns I mentioned above are wrong or inappropriate in and of themselves. I am saying they weren't considerations in David's relational ministry to the Lord, or to His people. His heart's intent (core motivation) established and influenced the context for the content he created and offered up sacrificially. In contemplating David's public reputation and recognition, keep these two verses in mind:

1 Samuel 13:14 says that the LORD "...*sought out a man after his own heart...*"

"...*[T]he sweet psalmist of Israel...*"
~2 Sam. 23:1

> **To the choirmaster. A psalm of David.**
> *The heavens declare the glory of God, and the sky above proclaims his handiwork. Day to day pours out speech, and night to night reveals knowledge. There is no speech, nor are there words, whose voice is not heard. Their voice goes out through all the earth, and their words to the end of the world. In them he has set a tent for the sun, which comes out like a bridegroom leaving his chamber, and, like a strong man, runs its course with joy. Its rising is from the end of the heavens, and its circuit to the end of them, and there is nothing hidden from its heat. The **law** of the Lord is perfect, reviving the soul; the **testimony** of the Lord is sure, making wise the simple; the **precepts** of the Lord are right, rejoicing the heart; the **commandment** of the Lord is pure, enlightening the eyes; the fear of the Lord is clean, enduring forever; the **rules** of the Lord are true, and righteous*

altogether. More to be desired are they than gold, even much fine gold; sweeter also than honey and drippings of the honeycomb. Moreover, by them is your servant warned; in keeping them there is great reward. Who can discern his errors? Declare me innocent from hidden faults. Keep back your servant also from presumptuous sins; let them not have dominion over me! Then I shall be blameless, and innocent of great transgression. **Let the words of my mouth and the meditation of my heart be acceptable in your sight, O Lord, my rock and my redeemer.**

~Psalm 19 emphasis added

In speaking of Dietrich Bonhoeffer, Bishop Chris Green says, "In his verse-by-verse commentary of Psalm 119 (which he didn't finish) he [Bonhoeffer] said that he considered it to be the most important work he would ever do."

"Knowledge comes through obedience. It's through obedience that we are led to all truth," (D. Bonhoeffer; see 1 Tim. 1:5).

Remember: Worship is obedience service, manifesting through self-sacrifice (Wayne-Speak; see Rom.12:1–2).

During this last stage of *love labor*, the Holy Ghost (yet again) placed more pertinent information in my path. The following article by David Guzik elevates Psalm 119 to the high level it deserves. The overall content is so compatible with (essential to) this portion of what you're reading, I could not exclude any of it. However, it's too long to use in full. In the article, Guzik quotes several others for their comments. He certainly deserves credit for his research, as do those whom he quotes. In order to include these pertinent portions of the article, I've chosen to break out each author's quote by highlighting them individually. So, I'm attributing the credit due them by acknowledging all their contributions herewith:

This long psalm deserves a long introduction. The author is unnamed; older commentators almost universally said it is a psalm of David, composed throughout his entire life. More modern commentators sometimes conclude that it is post-exilic, coming from the days of Nehemiah or Ezra. It may be that David was the author, but we can't say this with certainty, and it is not necessary to know; if it were important, God would have preserved the name of David to this psalm. No matter who the author was, it was likely written over some period of time and later compiled, because there is not a definite flow of thought from the beginning of the psalm to the end. The sections and verses are not like a chain, where one link is connected to the other, but like a string of pearls where each pearl has equal, but independent value.

Psalm 119 is arranged in an acrostic pattern. There are 22 letters in the Hebrew alphabet, and this psalm contains 22 units of 8 verses each. Each of the 22 sections is given a letter of the Hebrew alphabet, and each line in that section begins with that letter. The closest parallel to this pattern in Scripture is found in Lamentations 3, which is also divided into 22 sections, and a few other passages in the Hebrew Scriptures use an acrostic pattern.

Since this is a psalm glorifying God and His word, it refers to Scripture repeatedly. Psalm 119 is remarkable for how often it refers to God's written revelation, His word. It is referred to in almost every verse. The Masoretes (a group of Jewish scholars between the 6th and 10th centuries AD) said that the word of God is mentioned in every verse except Psalm 119:122. Other people analyze this differently (with disagreement about Psalm 119:84, 90, 121, 132). But Scripture is mentioned in at least 171 of the 176 verses.

In this psalm there are eight basic words used to describe the Scriptures, God's written revelation to us:

1. **Law** (torah, used 25 times in Psalm 119): "Its parent verb means 'teach' or 'direct'; therefore coming from God it means both 'law' and 'revelation.' It can be used of a single command or of a whole body of law." **(Derek Kidner)**

2. **Word** (dabar, used 24 times): The idea is of the spoken word, God's revealed word to man. "Proceeding from his mouth and revealed by him to us…" **(Matthew Poole)**

3. **Judgments** (mispatim, used 23 times): "…from shaphat, to judge, determine, regulate, order, and discern, because they judge concerning our words and works; show the rules by which they should be regulated; and cause us to discern what is right and wrong, and decide accordingly." **(Adam Clarke)**

4. **Testimonies** (edut/edot, used 23 times): This word is related to the word for witness. To obey His **testimonies** "…signifies loyalty to the terms of the covenant made between the Lord and Israel." **(Willem VanGemeren)**

5. **Commandments** (miswah/miswot, used 22 times): "This word emphasizes the straight authority of what is said…the right to give orders." **(Derek Kidner)**

6. **Statutes** (huqqim, used 21 times): The noun is derived from the root verb "engrave" or "inscribe"; the idea is the written word of God and the authority of His written word: "…declaring his authority and power of giving us laws." **(Matthew Poole)**

7. **Precepts** (piqqudim, used 21 times): "This is a word drawn from the sphere of an officer or overseer, a man who is responsible to look closely into a situation and take action…. So the word points

to the particular instructions of the Lord, as of one who cares about detail." **(Derek Kidner)**

8. **Word** (imrah, used 19 times): Imrah is similar in meaning to dabar, yet a different term. "The 'word' may denote anything God has spoken, commanded, or promised." **(Willem VanGemeren)**

The theme of the glory of Scripture is diligently explored in this psalm, but always in connection with God Himself. Derek Kidner remarks: "This untiring emphasis has led some to accuse the psalmist of worshipping the Word rather than the Lord; but it has been well remarked that every reference here to Scripture, without exception, relates it explicitly to its Author; indeed, every verse from 4 to the end is a prayer for affirmation addressed to Him. This is true piety: a love of God not desiccated by study but refreshed, informed and nourished by it."

"This wonderful psalm, from its great length, helps us to wonder at the immensity of Scripture. From its keeping to one subject it helps us to adore the unity of Scripture; for it is but one. Yet, from the many turns it gives to the same thought, it helps you to see the variety of Scripture.... Some have said that in it there is an absence of variety, but that is merely the observation of those who have not studied it. I weighed each word and looked at each syllable with lengthened meditation; and I bear witness that this sacred song has no tautology in it but is charmingly varied from beginning to end. Its variety is that of a kaleidoscope: from a few objects a boundless variation is produced. In the kaleidoscope you look once, and there is a strangely beautiful form. You shift the glass a very little, and another shape, equally delicate and beautiful, is before your eyes. So it is here." **(Charles Spurgeon)**

Being such a long psalm—and the longest chapter in the Bible—this psalm has been of great historical interest. There have been many lengthy works written on this psalm; one of them is by Thomas Manton, a Puritan preacher and writer, who wrote a three-volume work on Psalm 119. Each volume is between 500 and 600 pages, with a total of 1,677 pages. There are 190 chapters in his work, more than one chapter for each verse.

"Luther professed that he prized this Psalm so highly, that he would not take the whole world in exchange for one leaf of it." **(Charles Bridges)**

Some great people have memorized this whole psalm and found great blessing in doing so: John Ruskin (19th century British writer), William Wilberforce (19th century British politician who led the movement to abolish the slave trade in the British Empire), Henry Martyn (19th century pioneer missionary to India), and David Livingstone (19th century pioneer missionary to Africa).

Matthew Henry—the great 18th century Bible commentator—was introduced to Psalm 119 as a child. His father, Philip Henry, told his children to take one verse of Psalm 119 every morning to meditate on, and thereby go through the entire psalm twice in the year. Philip said to his children, "That will bring you to be in love with all the rest of the Scriptures." Perhaps that practice was why Matthew Henry loved the Bible so much that he wrote commentary that is used still today.

George Wishart was the Bishop of Edinburgh in the 17th century (not to be confused with another Scot by the same name who was martyred a century earlier). Wishart was condemned to death for his faith. But when he was on the scaffold, he made use of a custom that allowed the condemned person to choose one psalm to be sung, and he chose Psalm 119. Before two-thirds of the psalm had been sung, his pardon arrived, and his life was spared.

~Guzik, David
"Psalm 119: The Greatness and Glory of God's Word.
https://endurningword.com/bible-commentary/psalm-119/
Dec. 21, 2015

Concerning Franchised Worship

The first step in addressing this topic is to define *a franchise*:

A **franchise** is a business model where an entrepreneur (the franchisee) is granted the right to operate a business using the franchisor's trademark, products, services, and established systems.
~https://cmitfranchise.com/blog/what-is-a-franchise/

After four and a half decades of corporate ministry as a worship pastor and teaching Levite (2 Chron. 35:2–4), I find myself viewing the current dynamics with many congregations in America (and around the world) as being active examples of franchise service. To say this concerns me would be an understatement. However, my postulation here isn't to try and tackle that subject directly. I'll leave that to the reader to sort out—with the help of the Holy Ghost. What follows isn't meant as a judgment. No disrespect or condescension is intended. We *all* must continue to work through matters of salvation and reconciliation together, as best we can.

"...[W]ork out the salvation that God has given you with a proper sense of awe and responsibility. For it is God who is at work within you, giving you the will and the power to achieve his purpose,"

~Phil. 2:12–13, Phillips

Remember, this passage is written to a congregational collective of followers of Christ. Although it is to be implemented by individuals, it is (first and foremost) to be processed by groups at large. It is not a singular directive. Rather, it is a charge upon a group (or groups) of believers. The text isn't about you and Jesus. It's about us and our Lord, and Savior.

To clarify: I am not addressing denominational affiliations, church plants, or so-called satellite fellowship extensions. My observations are based on how the worship departments in many churches today seem designed to function, and how that affects the dynamics of theology and doctrine in their congregations. (For example: *Who writes the songs; where is the inspiration and creative impetus rooted; how is the material developed, introduced, and digested within the fellowships, etc.?*)

The further we move away from our historical foundations, the less stable our foundations become. In essence I'm asking two simple questions:

Why did David function as a worshipper the way he did?

Why do we?

Here's a connective causeway (a Biblical bridge) from where we've been traveling to where we're headed:

At the trailhead of the pathway that David traveled—the "holy highway" (Isa. 35:8–9)—there is a supply store where travelers can stock up before they set out. It's a storehouse of treasured goods. Inside, there is a kiosk with a sign hanging overhead that reads, "Language Resources." Just under it, there is an aphorism that says, "The New Testament is contained in the Old, and the Old Testament is explained in the New." While there, you can pick up a guide pamphlet with directional instructions to follow. A portion of it follows.

Treasures Old and New

"Therefore, every scribe who has been trained for the

136

kingdom of heaven is like a master of a house, who brings out of his treasure what is new and what is old,"
                                                              ~Mt. 13:52

I'll unpack a few words used there so that a clearer picture becomes visible:

Scribe: A writer, secretary, town clerk. From a word meaning a keeper of letters, notes, epistles, books, etc. The work is intended as a means of teaching, or learning.

Treasure: A deposit; wealth (literally or figuratively). From a work meaning to place in a designated position.

New: Freshness.

Old: Antique; not recent; worn out. From a word meaning retrocession; formerly; sometime since; ancient; a great while ago; in time past. From a word meaning oscillatory repletion; to make new; bring back once more; to repeat or do again. All of that can be considered as a form of *repristinating. (Strong's Bible Concordance)

When these meanings are applied to Matthew 13:52, they shed a brighter light on what's being directed to implement.

*Repristinating:** The same idea (or principle) is at work in Mark 2:22 which says, *"[N]o one puts new wine into old wineskins. If he does, the wine will burst the skins—and the wine is destroyed, and so are the skins. But new wine is for fresh wineskins."*

This text isn't about preference (new vs. old). That is often the way it is considered, taught on, or preached about. However, it is fundamentally about preservation—keeping/making both new and old available as needed or desired.

Bishop Joseph Garlington brought a teaching decades ago that gave me an entirely different perspective on how both sections of Scripture under consideration are to be appropriated and used (personally and corporately).

Old wineskins shouldn't necessarily be discarded due to their age. There is a process by which restoration to usefulness can take place. That process is called *repristinating (repristination)*. It means to bring back into functional service.

As I recall his narrative, it is as follows:

To restore old wineskins, there are three steps to be applied—in order, and over a reasonable time span:

1. The skins are soaked in fresh water.
2. Then, as they are drying out, they are to be pounded with wooden hammers on stones to work out the wrinkles they have developed through use.
3. Afterward, they are hand-rubbed with fresh oil to restore their suppleness to a flexible and viable condition.

Although the subject matter is different in Psalm 51:2, the practice of restoration and renewal is the same dynamic as expressed above. Take a moment to ponder that text: *"Wash me clean of my iniquity and cleanse me from my sin," (BSB).*

Linking those two Scriptural aspects together provides a much broader understanding of how this applies within the context of true worship.

Hanging Up Our Harps

> *By the rivers of Babylon, there we sat down and wept, when we remembered Zion. Upon the willows in the midst of it we hung our harps. For there our captors demanded of us songs, and our tormentors, jubilation, saying, "Sing for us one of the songs of Zion!"*
>
> ~Psalm 137:1–3 NASB

This is one of the most overlooked and under-considered passages in all of the scripture related to the *why* of worship. I'll provide a brief historical context from Charles Spurgeon for the content that's to follow:

> *This plaintive ode is one of the most charming compositions*

in the whole Book of Psalms for its poetic power. If it were not inspired it would nevertheless occupy a high place in poesy, especially the former portion of it, which is tender and patriotic to the highest degree. In the later verses (Ps. 137:7–9), we have utterances of burning indignation against the chief adversaries of Israel—an indignation as righteous as it was fervent. Let those find fault with it who have never seen their temple burned, their city ruined, their wives ravished, and after children slain; they might not, perhaps, be quite so velvet mouthed if they had suffered after this fashion. It is one thing to talk of the bitter feeling which moved captive Israelites in Babylon, and quite another thing to be captives ourselves under a savage and remorseless power, which knew not how to show mercy, but delighted in barbarities to the defenseless. The song is such as might fitly be *sung in the Jews' wailing place. It is a fruit of the Captivity in Babylon, and often has it furnished expression for sorrows which else had been unutterable. It is an odalisque Psalm within whose mild radiance there glows afire which strikes the beholder with wonder.

~Spurgeon, Charles. *A Treasury of David*

*Psalm 137 is known as a Song of Lament.

Looking at Lament

To expose the core of including songs of lament, allow me to relate some personal backstory. To accomplish that, I'll do two things. First, I encourage you to purchase and read *Reality, Grief, Hope* by Walter Brueggemann. It was published by Wm. B. Eerdmans Publishing Co. in 2014, but it has grown much more meaningful and relevant over the last decade. *If* you decide to follow up on my suggestion, pay close attention to the chapter entitled, "Grief Amid Denial."

The second thing to note is that the core which lies at the heart of this portion of my postulating is empathy. The word *empathy* isn't found in Scripture as such. Its meaning, according to Webster's New Collegiate Dictionary, is the capacity for participation in another's feelings or ideas. Biblically speaking, the closest word to that concept would likely be *mercy*. Perhaps the very best example of empathic mercy is shown to humankind in the words that Jesus uttered upon the cross, *"Forgive them Father, for they know not what they do," (Lu. 23:34).*

Although the word *mercy* is not mentioned in the verse below, it shows how it is outworked (imparted) by God, directly to those who need it:

> *For thus says the One who is high and lifted up, who inhabits eternity, whose name is Holy: "I dwell in the high and holy place, and also with him who is of a contrite and lowly spirit, to revive the spirit of the lowly, and to revive the heart of the contrite."*
>
> ~Isaiah 57:15

The Fathers, coming down—so to speak—is directly linked to how we approach Him in humility and contrition (our brokenness). He enters the despair, suffering, and pain of our fallen humanity as a direct result of His Sovereign, Divine, and Providential mercy toward us (see 1 Peter 5:6).

Side note: Spurgeon's commentary on Psalm 137 clearly narrates how such empathic mercy can/should underpin how we extend ourselves to others in their time(s) of need. (Also see Heb. 4:16.)

Now, own to my personal backstory…

Beginning in 2004, my wife and I (along with various ministry teams) were active in three-to-six-week short-term ministry on the African continent. For almost twenty years we taught, preached, and led worship (corporately and in seminars). Our *sphere of influence* reached across five nations, and linked us to dozens of churches, and hundreds of people (see 2 Cor. 10:13–16).

One event relates directly to Psalm 137 and the outworking I experienced in Harare, Zimbabwe, during an evening service in 2006. Here's a brief remembrance…

We were gathered in Warren Park, outside of Harare, during very stark times. The national economy was in a major downslide, headed toward an unprecedented collapse. The sanctuary of this church had yet to be built, so we met outside in what's commonly referred to as a Tabernacle—consisting of a cement slab floor and a corrugated metal roof held up by support beams made of small, debarked trees. It did have electric wiring for bare light bulbs, but they only worked when the electricity did—which was anybody's guess.

The only thing in abundance was a lack of *everything*.

Into that cultural dynamic, we had just finished a time of corporate praise and worship (African style). It was a fantastic experience, gathered there under the darkness of the African sky. Following that, a couple of announcements were made, just prior to my time to preach. Then, just before I stood up to walk toward the tiny stage, the Holy Ghost spoke to me and said that I should disregard my prepared message, disregard my notes, and say what He gave me to share.

As I stepped to the mic and turned to address the congregation, all the power throughout the entire township went out. It was silent, still, and very, very dark. Within less than thirty seconds the entire situation changed. Those in attendance were prepared for what was happening, since such things are a way of life in so-called "Third World" countries. Candles suddenly were being lit by some who were seated inside. Others who were standing outside and around the Tabernacle also began to light their candles. The PA was out, but that didn't matter. We could see each other's faces, and I was there to preach. So, that's exactly what I began to do. Since I had scrapped my planned sermon, the only thing stirring in my spirit was a text I'd been meditating on for several days. That text was Psalm 137, and so I began to speak what the Lord gave me in *real time*.

I preached the first six verses. (The other verses didn't seem appropriate to the current circumstances of the evening, or the overall conditions that the people [and the nation] were living in.) As I shared, I had no idea what to do but encourage the people to not lose their song(s). That's really all that I knew to say. The more I unpacked those verses, the more tears began to flow. When I tried to explain how their spirit of patient endurance and longsuffering was impacting me, the more they wept.

It was at that moment that I knew I was witnessing a reenactment of the historical events expressed in the Psalm. The striking difference was that there were no harps, willow trees, or captors speaking condescendingly at those gathered in yielded adoration. It was (and still is) an amazing memory to recall. Besides the personal, heart-felt impact of that evening, I came away with two other gifts—this testimony and the song that follows:

Song of Zion

~Ps. 137

Bowed down and broken, with burdens too heavy to bear
With fears unspoken, afraid I (we) would die of despair
Still there was one light that shined out in the darkness
And that one light was all I (we) needed to see

So I (we) will sing one more song of Zion
Yes, I (we) will sing this song to the glory of God
And I (we) will sing one more song of deliverance
I'll (we'll) sing till He comes
I'll (we'll) sing till He comes

By the Babylon River, we sat down and wept for our home
It was there that our captors demanded we sing them our song
Still there was one light that shined out in the darkness
And that one light was all we needed to see
~W. Berry, See & Say Songs, BMI, circa 2006

Note to reader: These lectures by Walter Brueggemann fit with everything I've just addressed in the preceding section. I highly recommend conducting a search on YouTube.com to access these presentations:

Walter Brueggemann Need for Lament (Psalms)

Lecture 1 "Orientation"—Walter Brueggemann

Lecture 2 Disorientation: Faith in the Depths—Walter Brueggemann

Lecture 3 New Orientation: Faith as Gift and as Impossibility—Walter Brueggemann

Silent Worship

As I wind down my ponderings on Worship, it is Holy Week 2025. The following seems particularly appropriate to include here, toward the end of all I've been addressing. Read it as you ponder what you've just read regarding Psalm 137:

A phrase in the Hillsong United song "So Will I (100 Billion X)" has me pondering... how do rocks cry out in silence, and is that something that should apply to me? One way of considering what this means is to keep in mind that there is an aspect of silent worship that is Biblically based, but rarely incorporated into our so-called contemporary congregational services.

Note to reader: For more regarding silence in worship, please consider *Encounters with Silence* by Karl Rahner, St. Augustine's Press, 1999.

By faith Jacob, when he was a dying—Genesis 47:31; Genesis 48:1-20. That is, when he was about to die. He saw his death near when he pronounced this blessing on Ephraim and Manasseh, the sons of Joseph.

And worshipped, leaning upon the top of his staff— This is an exact quotation from the Septuagint in Genesis 47:31. The English version of that place is, "and

Israel bowed himself upon the bed's head," which is a proper translation, in the main, of the word הַמִּטָּה miTTah. That word, however, with different vowel points—הַמַּטֶּה maTTeh, means a branch, a bough, a rod, a staff, and the translators of the Septuagint have so rendered it. The Masoretic points are of no authority, and either translation, therefore, would be proper. The word rendered "head" in Genesis 47:31—"bed's head"—שְׁאַר ro'sh, means properly head, but may there mean the top of anything, and there is no impropriety in applying it to the head or top of a staff. The word rendered in Genesis 47:31 as "bowed"—וַיִּשְׁתַּחוּ—implies properly the idea of "worshipping." It is bowing, or prostration for the purpose of worship or homage.

~Barnes' Notes on the Bible

Out of all the content of the Torah that the writer of Hebrews could have used to exemplify worship—under the New Testament covenant—He mentions the story narrated in Genesis 47:31. That being his choice, I'll bear witness to it as well with one word—AMEN!

The heavens declare the glory of God, and the sky above proclaims his handiwork. Day to day pours out speech, and night to night reveals knowledge. There is no speech, nor are there words, whose voice is not heard. Their voice goes out through all the earth, and their words to the end of the world.
~Psalm 19:1–4

For his invisible attributes, namely, his eternal power and divine nature, have been clearly perceived, ever since the creation of the world, in the things that have been made. So they are without excuse.
~Romans 1:20

The Pursuit of Presence

In the matter of seeking for Presence…

Old Testament Text: Psalm 139:7–12

Where shall I go from your Spirit? Or where shall I flee from your presence? If I ascend to heaven, you are there! If I make my bed in Sheol, you are there! If I take the wings of the morning and dwell in the uttermost parts of the sea, even there your hand shall lead me, and your right hand shall hold me. If I say, "Surely the darkness shall cover me, and the light about me be night," even the darkness is not dark to you; the night is bright as the day, for darkness is as light with you.

New Testament Text: 1 Corinthians 3:16

Do you not know that you are God's temple and that God's Spirit dwells in you?

So, why is Presence important?

I'll begin with where I want to end up, and then backtrack to the start:

> *"For it was fitting that He, for whom and by whom all things exist, in bringing many sons to glory, should make the founder of their salvation *perfect through suffering,"*
> ~Heb. 2:10

*Perfect—Complete; fulfilled; consecrated. (Strong's Bible Concordance)

This verse provides a self-contained synopsis of the history of God's overall plan for humankind. It tells us who's responsible for all things that exist—Creator God (see Jn. 1:3); what His reason was/is for doing what's taken place—establishing a Kingdom citizenry (1 Peter 2:9); identifies the founder (or source)

146

of reconciliation, leading to redemption—Jesus Christ (2 Cor. 5:18-21); and establishes that suffering was a key component that brought His assignment to completion: *"nevertheless, not my will but Thine be done," (Lu. 22:42)*. It does all of that, using only thirty words!

If you continue to unpack the verse, you'll find multiple dozens of verses that expand and expound upon what it says. I find it interesting that I've never heard this verse taught on or preached about. Curious, to say the least.

The dynamic events it mentions share a common aspect. Presence is essential as the foundational underpinning for any of those things to have taken place. You could say that Presence made everything possible. I'll explain what I mean with a brief overview:

Biblically speaking, the creation story shows us an interchange between/among the Trinity. Genesis 1:26 says, *"Let us make man in our image."* In doing so, we see that the Father, Son, and Holy Ghost are relational. They share an interconnected union with one another. And, based on that union, their desire to expand relationship to include others took place.

So, man, and woman (humankind) began. That in turn prompted the actions and events that were to make *bringing many sons to glory* possible. That would have been undoable without having a starting point in time on earth. That starting point took place when God's Presence showed up.

The first manifestation of active Presence took place in the Garden. It is described in Genesis 3:8 which states, *"Then the man and his wife heard the voice of the LORD God walking in the garden in the breeze of the day," (BSB)*.

For God to have been heard walking, He had to be present on earth. That being the case, my initial response to the question of *"Why is Presence important?"* is that without it, nothing that has happened since the events in the Garden could have happened. Everything thereafter is (wait for it)…history.

Vision

I have a vision of a world yet to come
Where only peace and sweet release
Flow from the Master's throne

I have a vision of the Kingdom from above
Coming down in light, making all things bright
And bathing the world in love

BRIDGE:
It's for you to share, it's for those who dare
To believe what they cannot see
There's a choice to make, there's a path to take
That leads from here to eternity

I have a vision, there are those who share this dream
As the day draws near they prepare to hear
The sound of the trumpets ring
At that call we'll all bow and sing
Proclaiming Jesus Christ as King
                    ~W. Berry, See & Say Songs, circa 1985

Also Available From

Wayne Berry
Pondering(s)
Pondering(s) Too
Particular Pondering(s)
Questing: A Kingdom Recalibration

Each of those books served as narrative construction sites upon which pathways (roadways) were built. Those pathway(s) provided road maps of a sort, as part of the *questing* I continue to navigate. They've helped to guide me from where I was to where I'm headed. They are available through several online outlets.

Seek and find.

Also Available From

WordCrafts Press

Created for Someone
by Mario Villella

A Pastor's Secrets
by Ronnie Meek

God in the Commonplace
by Beverly Clopton

Illuminations
by Paula K. Parker

What's the Big Idea?
by Robert G. Lee